How You Can Use The Technique of CREATIVE IMAGINATION

by Roy Eugene Davis

Publisher/CSA Press
Lakemont, Georgia/30552

Twenty-Sixth Printing 1987

Library of Congress Catalog Card No. 74-75315

International Standard Book Number 0-87707-133-0

Published by CSA Press, the literature department of Center for Spiritual Awareness, Box 7, Lake Rabun Road, Lakemont, Georgia 30552.

PRINTED IN THE UNITED STATES OF AMERICA

Contents

HOW THIS BOOK CAN HELP YOU

Many readers call this the *miracle book* because it has been so helpful. Improved health, better social relationships, greater evidence of prosperity, and even a welcome expansion of consciousness has been reported. This comes as no surprise to me, because I have been on a daily working relationship with these methods and principles for years and I know the laws of consciousness are exact and dependable.

I would suggest that you use this book as a daily guide until the principles become so much a part of you that you no longer have to take conscious thought to cooperate with them. Reading is not enough; there must be personal application so that one proves out what is mentally assimilated. The challenge is, "can we take these ideas and principles and. use them to work needed change in our lives, and transformation in the world?"

One thing is certain, *man can alter his circumstances and change his lot in life by intentionally controlling his mental attitude and states of consciousness.* Every prophet has proclaimed this to be true, every successful person bears witness to it, now it is your opportunity to prove it for yourself.

You cannot possibly fail.

Roy Eugene Davis
Day of the New Year, 1974

"Are you in earnest? Seize this very minute;
What you can do, or dream you can, begin it;
Boldness has genius, power and magic in it.
Only engage and then the mind grows heated;
Begin, and then the work will be completed."

—Goethe

"Man may attract and direct any force of the Universe
by making himself a fit receptacle for it, establishing a
connection with it, and arranging conditions so that its
nature compels it to flow through him."

—Anonymous

Chapter One

YOU CAN DO IT

There is a power which controls and regulates the universe and we can learn to cooperate with it. When we do, we experience riches of a practical nature and joys most people seldom even dream possible. To move into a working relationship with this power is not a selfish act, for as we learn to work with the principles which undergird nature herself, the power flows to benefit the world.

I believe you can do any reasonable thing you feel led to do, have any reasonable experience you want to have, and be the kind of person you were really designed to be. I use the word *reasonable* in order to point out the necessity of being realistic, and of working with innate capacities as well as natural and social laws.

The principles you will learn to use are simple to understand, and virtually guarantee success. In fact, the key technique which forms the basis for this treatise has, itself, been referred to as "the success system that never fails to bring results." The presentation is simple. I suggest you use this book as a working manual. Underline the text, make notes in the margins, apply the principles and take the ideas into daily experience. In this way you will be involved with life itself instead of being an armchair philosopher, or a planner whose goals are to be reached "eventually," when conditions change, the breaks come, or when the time is right.

The Basic Premise

In order to correctly utilize the principles which follow we will have to clearly understand the basic premise which makes all of the techniques and methods valid: *the world and all it contains is formed of one basic substance.* This is not a new concept. It has been understood, and taught, for thousands of years. One basic substance is formed variously as our world of names and forms. Some teachers refer to this basic substance as the fabric of nature, and the components are: time; space; light particles; and creative energy.

A characteristic of this substance is that it takes the impress of thought. We can, by impressing our thoughts upon universal cause-substance, form it according to our just desire. The world around us is the result of cosmic patterns expressing through universal cause-substance; and we modify our environment by impressing this same substance with our personal thoughts, or mental pictures.

What a person becomes, or does with his life, is largely the effect of his conscious or subconscious mental picturing. Even if we attribute present-time experiences to karma, we are admitting that today's experiences are the effect of previous decisions, or mentally accepted concepts. By controlling mental imagery we can cooperate with nature and participate in planning the pattern for future experience.

Events of the past need not control us now. The planets need not unduly influence us. Economic trends need not make, or break, us. We are not destined to be controlled by friends, associates, or those who would run our lives. The life we live is the unique result of our personal relationship with the universe; once we learn how to work with the *regulating power* and *controlling intelligence* which is ever about the cosmic duties.

The Power of Decision

Hundreds of inspirational books have been published, with millions of copies distributed over the years. Yet, only a small percentage of all readers ever personally apply the principles and experience any degree of dramatic change for the better. Why is this? Because most people are content to remain in a routine pattern. Most people cannot make a decision. They are afraid of the consequences, or unsure of themselves when it comes to the point where they will have to follow-through with constructive action. Many are not fulfilled, but they are "comfortable" and getting along alright. They don't want to make waves, upset others with whom they are associated, or initiate action which will require courage to justify. Many counselors and management spokesmen have come to the conclusion that only five-percent of the population are possessed of sufficient mental ability, self-discipline and "the will to follow through" to actually become permanently self-determined and self-sufficient. Therefore, the first thing for you to do is: decide *now* that you are going to be one of the few who make up that small percentage of successful people.

Goals give direction in life. When we have worthwhile goals we also have a sense of meaning and purpose. To set goals we have to be clear-minded and be able to make decisions. Not all decisions will be correct, but practice gives us the opportunity to become proficient. Once decided on a course of action, all of our thoughts and energies become mobilized and focused upon definite goals.

Experience Enters Through the Mental Attitude

Self-acceptance is vital, everything else follows. Without self-acceptance there can be no confidence, therefore no courage to act. Self-acceptance leads to self-confidence. Self-confidence leads to decision-making and to purposeful action, the success-cycle then becomes complete. If you feel that you are not worthy of being healthy, prosperous, and creatively free and expressive, do some inner work on yourself and get rid of the negative thought patterns which keep you in bondage. We are worthy of fulfillment, and fulfillment is not so much a matter of our having to earn it, as it is to *accept* it.

What are our thoughts and opinions of others? Do we bless others and wish for their happiness and success? Or, are we prone to be envious, resentful, or even competitive? Occasionally a person will abide by all of the rules which usually guarantee success, and still fail. At such a time we ask: "Do you believe it is possible for others to fail (have problems, be ill, have accidents, etc.)?" The answer will be, "Yes." We may think positive for ourselves and yet retain negative thoughts about others. The law then is: *"That which I can believe true for others, can also be true for me."* Mental pictures are impersonal. Any mental picture which is retained in the mind will tend to externalize. This is the real reason why we are counseled to love our enemies, do good to those who would persecute us and pray for those who would wrongly use, or take advantage, of us. To harbor negative thoughts and feelings, no matter what the attempt at self-justification, is destructive and contrary to our avowed ideal of expressing prosperity and fulfillment.

Let us rid ourselves once and forever of self-limiting concepts, attitudes and feelings. Look upon nature, see how lavish and wondrously beautiful she is! Incredible energy is ceaselessly at work, pouring out an infinite variety of life forms. Energy is not created, nor is it destroyed; it flows from appearance to appearance. It animates forms and holds the pattern of the form itself. When life is balanced and all its parts are in harmony, fulfillment and synchronized action is automatic.

There are plenty of natural resources in the world,

and all living beings can know peace and plenty if creative intelligence is used in the management of these resources. A truly free person thinks in terms of using things with wisdom, for specific purposes, and not in terms of exploiting anyone or anything. We are stewards of the resources of the world. We may claim temporary ownership but we are really only entrusted with the wise use of things.

If we become compulsive owners we usually become possessed by the very things we thought were under our dominion. If we compulsively reject the things of the world we will not be capable of function. The middle path is suggested. The key is to move freely through life and be "in the world but not of it," as the great teachers suggest.

Remember:

1. There is a power which controls and regulates the universe and we can learn to cooperate with it.
2. The world and all it contains is formed of one basic substance.
3. Mental pictures externalize as circumstances.
4. Decisions mobilize energies and focus concentration.
5. Mental attitude is the "window" through which experience enters.
6. We are but stewards of the goods of the world.

Practical Application

1. Before going to the next chapter, resolve within yourself to use the principles recommended in this book, day by day. Otherwise, it will be just one more inspirational book which is scanned, thought about for a short time and laid aside. Try not to go past a word, phrase or concept without understanding what is read. Use a dictionary if necessary; but be sure the written word is crystal clear. Then, use intuition and discernment to "read between the lines" to arrive at the state of consciousness which produced the book in the first place.

2. The basic principles herein explained are important and can be understood. If some of the concepts are new to you, examine them carefully. Remember, they have been useful to millions of successful people. *You have the power to discern.*

3. All of the disciplines and techniques are useful, but the most subtle one of all, and the one which will take the greatest attention and care, is that of learning to maintain a positive and wholesome mental attitude at all times.

Use Any Blank Pages in This Book
for Your Own Notes

NOTES

"Ah, Love! could thou and I with Fate
   conspire
To grasp this sorry Scheme of Things
   entire,
Would we not shatter it to bits—and
   then
Re-mould it nearer to the Heart's Desire!"
                    —Rubaiyat of Omar Khayyam
                         Edward Fitzgerald

"Whatsoever things are pure, just, lovely, of good re-
port, think on these things."

Chapter Two

CLEARING THE FIELD

The game of life can be joyous and rewarding if we play according to nature's rules. There is nothing wrong about living fully on the earth plane, for the physical universe is as much an expression of life as are the more subtle energy realms which support it. Our desires and needs determine our sphere of action, and we are undoubtedly here because this is where we can best come to terms with ourselves and with life.

Let us think in terms of learning how to render useful service to others so we can leave the world a better place than it was when we first came to it. Let us resolve to live simply and with high ideals. Some philosophers suggest that our present life condition is the arena where we enact a personal drama in order to learn more, and to meet the tests which life presents to all who would seek out the inmost secrets. Again, the attitude is important; we should face the prospect with enthusiasm, knowing that we are certain to receive more than we can ever hope to give, for this is the way life deals with people. We have everything to gain by wholeheartedly participating, and only failure to experience by not doing so. In fact, upon careful examination of the possibilities: we have no other real choice! We can put it off; but we must eventually enter into the evolutionary stream and become involved with the process of growth and maturity.

Charting Your Cours

In order to become totally invol
you obtain a large notebook, and k
place when not using it. In this note
a *daily guide* and *planner*, write
near and distant future. This will cl
and enable you to be honest with
your goals and analyze your motives
to do the things you have set forth
Are they practical? Useful? Will th
well as others? Are they within reach

Another part of your notebook c
thoughts, reflections and ideas. Here
velop new themes and possibilities
beginning to flow through the mind i

Analyze yourself. List your st
weaknesses. Resolve to correct
Adjust your attitude, acquire neede
perience, do whatever it is you nee
well informed and capable. Collect
ful people, begin to associate with do
time with non-doers. Attune your
creative and action-oriented people
tion attune yourself to universal
and be an open channel through wh
dom can flow into expression.

Read books, take courses if
mainly, *apply* the principles in yo
the reading and study will be usele
in the fires of daily experience. T
thinkers and speakers; there are
producing doers! If something is wo
the timing is right, do it now! Be
With proper timing we expend less
accomplished.

"Ah, Love! could thou and I with Fate
    conspire
To grasp this sorry Scheme of Things
    entire,
Would we not shatter it to bits—and
    then
Re-mould it nearer to the Heart's Desire!"
                    —Rubaiyat of Omar Khayyam
                        Edward Fitzgerald

"Whatsoever things are pure, just, lovely, of good re-
port, think on these things."

NOTES

Chapter Two

CLEARING THE FIELD

The game of life can be joyous and rewarding if we play according to nature's rules. There is nothing wrong about living fully on the earth plane, for the physical universe is as much an expression of life as are the more subtle energy realms which support it. Our desires and needs determine our sphere of action, and we are undoubtedly here because this is where we can best come to terms with ourselves and with life.

Let us think in terms of learning how to render useful service to others so we can leave the world a better place than it was when we first came to it. Let us resolve to live simply and with high ideals. Some philosophers suggest that our present life condition is the arena where we enact a personal drama in order to learn more, and to meet the tests which life presents to all who would seek out the inmost secrets. Again, the attitude is important; we should face the prospect with enthusiasm, knowing that we are certain to receive more than we can ever hope to give, for this is the way life deals with people. We have everything to gain by wholeheartedly participating, and only failure to experience by not doing so. In fact, upon careful examination of the possibilities: we have no other real choice! We can put it off; but we must eventually enter into the evolutionary stream and become involved with the process of growth and maturity.

Charting Your Course

In order to become totally involved I suggest that you obtain a large notebook, and keep it in a private place when not using it. In this notebook, which will be a *daily guide* and *planner*, write your goals for the near and distant future. This will clarify your thinking and enable you to be honest with yourself. Examine your goals and analyze your motives. Why do you want to do the things you have set forth in your notebook? Are they practical? Useful? Will they benefit you, as well as others? Are they within reach?

Another part of your notebook can be used for idle thoughts, reflections and ideas. Here, you begin to develop new themes and possibilities while they are just beginning to flow through the mind into concrete form.

Analyze yourself. List your strengths and your weaknesses. Resolve to correct your weaknesses. Adjust your attitude, acquire needed education or experience, do whatever it is you need to do to become well informed and capable. Collect stories of successful people, begin to associate with doers and spend less time with non-doers. Attune yourself mentally with creative and action-oriented people. Through meditation attune yourself to universal creative intelligence and be an open channel through which power and wisdom can flow into expression.

Read books, take courses if you need to; but, mainly, *apply* the principles in your own life! All of the reading and study will be useless if it is not tested in the fires of daily experience. The world is full of thinkers and speakers; there are only a few result-producing doers! If something is worth doing now, and the timing is right, do it now! Be sure of the timing. With proper timing we expend less energy and more is accomplished.

We Are Only Self-Limited

Most people are limited by their own thinking patterns and by their emotional problems. Do you blame the past? Do you blame others who didn't understand you, didn't treat you well, or didn't do their part in a business relationship? Do you blame your parents? Your teachers? Government? Are you failure-prone, or success oriented? Do you harbor resentment, guilt or sneaking suspicion? Are you afraid of real or imaginary threats? Are you prejudiced, self-righteous or vain? These are all distortions on the mental-emotional level which are sure to inhibit the free expression of creative intelligence.

Short term goals are important because with them we can become immediately involved with the life process. Short term goals are usually fairly easy to reach and thus we receive early reinforcement of our intentions. We are rewarded for positive action and this creates a positive mental attitude, builds confidence and tends to neutralize failure patterns imprinted in the subconscious. The memories we have recorded on the subconscious level monitor our thoughts and actions. If we are loaded with negative memory-patterns we are somewhat paralyzed because we are afraid to act again for fear of failure. If our memory-patterns are, for the most part, the result of successes and degrees of fulfillment, we will be conditioned to the ideal of success and personal enrichment. It is literally true that success brings more success, and failure leads to failure. People who study failure patterns too much tend to become experts on the subject of failure, but not experts on success cycles. Success-oriented men and women are possessed of such magnetism, intuition and powers of perception that they are almost always forced to greater heights. But, one must begin; and then continue without wavering.

What Does Life Promise For You?

Yes, to what do you look forward, in this incarnation? What is important? Does life have meaning and purpose, as you see it? Our goals will vary according to our maturity. Some young people are driven by the desire for fast money, security, or things to use and possess. Others seek fame or recognition. Still others want to do something extraordinary, even if it is done in relative solitude. Goals vary; according to maturity, need, experience or prior conditioning.

At one time or another we have all asked: "Surely, there must be more to life than just paying the bills and providing food and shelter for the body—isn't there?" Money, possessions, human relations: these are not ends in themselves. Money without purpose is useless, possessions without function are a waste of investment, and human relationships without attunement and meaning are boring.

Essential to success in life are: *self-discipline, study of relative matters, contemplation, and an attitude of alert participation with life as an organic entity.* Discipline assures a conservation of energy and an intelligent directing of thought and motion. Study provides useful information, as well as inspiration and motivation. Contemplation affords time for unobstructed contact with universal forces. Alert participation is evidence of mental-emotional health and of spiritual maturity.

There is absolutely no reason why any man or woman who is reasonably intelligent should not be able to use known principles of thought, feeling, and action in such a way as to quickly step free from the past and move into the glorious present. *Here* and *now* is rich and abundant life. But, we must act decisively if we are to reap the harvest.

Cause and Effect are One

If a person can be made to feel certain emotions, and experience specific mental attitudes as a result of an environmental condition, *the reverse can also be true.* Cause and effect are one. *If we can be the effect of our environment, what is to prevent our environment from being the effect of our mental and emotional states?* It works both ways. Most people are effect, instead of cause. When we allow our environment to cause us to react, we are being the effect of our environment. When we assume the responsibility of either modifying the environment, or learning to live with it, we are no longer effect. We are then, either cause (of change) or we are part of the harmonious whole. Not all environmental conditions need to be changed; some need only to be gotten along with, without inner resistance.

The key to being *cause,* instead of effect, is to learn to control mental pictures and this is effectively done as a result of regular practice of a simple, but powerful, technique.

Remember:

1. The game of life can be rewarding and joyous.
2. Chart your course daily with the aid of a personal notebook.
3. The only limitations are self-limitations.
4. Discipline assures a conservation of energy and an intelligent directing of thought and motion.
5. Cause and effect are one.

Practical Application

Here are a few questions to ask yourself. Transfer these to your private notebook if you like. Be honest, and where change is required, begin now with a positive attitude.

1. What is my greatest strength?

2. What is my major weakness?

3. What is my major fear?

4. What is my highest hope or secret dream?

5. What was my greatest mistake?

6. What was my most noble deed?

7. Do I truly want to serve others?

8. Do I really forgive others and wish them well?

9. What would I most like to erase from my memory?

10. With the opportunity, what would I try to do better?

11. Do I always tell the truth?   Am I truthful with myself?

12. Am I practical and realistic or am I a daydreamer?

13. Am I really as I appear to others? What is the truth?

14. Whom do I love most of all?

15. Do I hate anyone? Why?

16. Do I fear anyone? Why?

17. Who has been the greatest influence in my life?

18. What are my major goals? Why?

19. How can I achieve them most efficiently?

20. If I have failed in the past, why have I?

21. Am I ready to leave this world without regret? Why, or why not?

22. Do I really make proper use of my time, energy, talents, mental powers and money? If not, why not?

23. Am I serious about living a creative life or am I just playing around?

24. Am I truly the person I want to be, and am I really and truly doing the best I can with my life?

By transferring these questions to your notebook you can allow more space for detailed explanations. This is for the purpose of making things clear in your own mind and helping you to become honest with yourself in relationship to life and living.

NOTES

NOTES

"But I have long had the feeling, which this study has matured to conviction, that Fancy and Imagination are not two powers at all, but one. The valid distinction which exists between them lies, not in the materials with which they operate, but in the degree of intensity of the operant power itself. Working at high tension the imaginative energy assimilates and transmutes; keyed low, the same energy aggregates and yokes together those images which at its highest pitch, it merges indissolubly into one."

—*The Road to Xanadu*
John Livingston Lowes

"Be still and know that you are that which you desire to be, and you will never have to search for it."
—*Neville*

Chapter Three

THE TECHNIQUE

We now arrive at the technique itself; how to use it, how it works, and what it can mean to you and your world. This procedure is the simple key you can use to make all reasonable dreams come true.

Webster's New Collegiate Dictionary gives this explanation: "*Imagination* 1. The Act or power of imagining; formation of mental images or objects not present to the senses, especially of those never perceived in their entirety; hence, mental synthesis of new ideas from elements experienced separately."

During uncontrolled moments we often daydream, and gather elements of a theme to form a casual mental arena of escape from sense-perceived conditions. Creative imagination is the result of *controlled* mental picturing, and has a positive effect on one's environment.

Fancy, or daydreaming, assembles mental ingredients; imagination gives definite form and exerts a creative force in the direction of manifestation. Read the words of Ralph Waldo Emerson: "Man surrounds himself with the true image of himself. Every spirit builds itself a house and beyond its world a heaven. Know then that the world exists for you. For you the phenomenon is perfect. What we are, that only can we see. All that Adam had, all that Caesar could, you have and can do. Adam called his house heaven and earth. Caesar called his house Rome; you perhaps call yours a cobbler's trade; a hundred acres of land, or a scholar's garret. Yet line for line, point for point, your dominion is as great as theirs, though without fine name. Build therefore your own world. As fast as you conform your life to the pure idea of your mind, that will unfold its great proportion."

How to Practice

The technique of creative imagination is simple to practice. All it takes is the discipline to spend a few minutes alone each day and to control the picture-forming nature of the mind. Remember, mental pictures tend to externalize as events and experiences, so when we control mental pictures we are able to control experiences and events yet to come. Just as the present is the effect of past causes, so the future will be the effect of present causes.

1. Relax in a quiet place where you will not be disturbed. Either recline on the bed or in an easy chair. Let the mind become clear and open. Be aware in the present; with no memories of the past, or desires for the future to interfere with the creative process to come.

2. In your mind's eye, assemble all of the items necessary to create a finished picture of an ideal condition you wish to experience. In other words, create a mental picture of yourself living in a state or condition desired. Or, create a scene, in your mind's eye, that would imply the fulfillment of your desire.

3. Now, make it a present-time fact to your mind and to your feeling nature; by thinking and feeling the fulfilled picture to be a *now* reality. Get the feeling of *then* (the point in future-time) as being right *now*. The subconscious mind merely accepts whatever is given to it; it does not know the difference between a memory pattern of an objective event and a subjective one—that is, an event experienced in the three-dimensional world versus one experienced purely in imagina-

tion. By thinking and feeling as though the event or experience desired were *now real*, you are able to encourage a change in subconscious acceptance, as well as neutralize feelings of lack, limitation, failure and inability to function. You are, in fact, becoming the person you have always wanted to be; and this will enable you to function at that new level and experience all things consistent with it.

4. The final step is to sink more deeply into a relaxed mental state; or even go to sleep for a while. The reason for this is to insure the memory of the imagined event is firmly recorded in mind and consciousness. If we stop the imaginative experience and move directly into a routine pattern of living, we may be forced from the imaginative feeling experience to a contrasting sense perception experience; and thus our controlled imagery will be neutralized and rendered less than effective.

Be clear about the process; we are not kidding ourselves, or living in an unreal world, when we use creative imagination. We are, instead, taking charge of our mental patterns in order to put order in our lives. Most people do not control mental images, feelings, or actions. Through discipline we can so control our thoughts and feelings that our actions automatically follow in line. Also, we attract to us all that is required for prosperous and natural living. As we move in an ocean of mind-substance which is responsive to our mental impressions, this substance takes form according to the pattern we hold before It. This is why controlled imagination is the key to controlling destiny.

After we become skilled we will not have to set aside much time for the practice of the technique. We will be able to so control thoughts and feelings that we can make needed adjustments in a few moments.

Now, back to the procedure, and some of the fine points. Let us assume your present desire is for a place in which to live; and it must be within your means,

conveniently located, comfortable and attractive. Do
not look around and finally settle on what is available.
Do not grumble, complain and display negative attitudes. Just be still, in a quiet place, and clear the mind.
The mind will clear itself if we relax, with an objective
attitude, and let thoughts drift. Then, create a picture
in your mind's eye of an ideal home situation. See the
spacious rooms, the attractive view, the furniture,
rugs, lamps and whatever else will be there. Have a
trusted friend in the mental picture and have him say,
"I'm so glad to see you happily located and at such a
fair price!" Then, *respond with gratitude and a
feeling of fulfillment, as you would were it actually taking place in the objective realm.* This is what I mean
by making a desire-picture real to the senses. When we
feel it to be real, it is no longer just a passing mental
picture, it is an experience.

What If You Cannot Visualize?

"But," you say, "what if I cannot visualize very
well?" Anyone can learn to visualize, with practice.
However, to save time, instead of visualizing just enter
into the calm state and hold a mental conversation with
a trusted friend; a conversation that would imply the
fulfillment of your desire, with all the feelings of
reality. *Inward hearing,* and actual *feeling,* are the
keys to success in this procedure.

Success is not demonstrated as a result of our imi-
tating the mere actions of successful people, but by our
own control of mental pictures and personal feelings.
What we hold steady in imagination must eventually
reflect in our outer world, for this is the law of mind in
action. The state of consciousness we sustain will even
devise the means which are best suited, so that, line for
line and point for point, the inner world matches the
outer one.

The key is to *think and feel from the end result, as it is certain to be;* even before it comes into objective manifestation. States of consciousness determine environmental conditions once we understand how to co-operate with the creative law. If we do not learn to co-operate with the creative law, we are fated to go through life being the effect of external causes, or the superior goal-setting ability of others whose lives overshadow our own.

We must move forward into our psychological assumptions, otherwise we drift without purpose. By controlling assumptions we give direction and purpose to our life pattern. When we live in thought and feeling, *as we would like our external life to be,* we transcend the seeming limitations of time and space and begin to create a place for ourselves in a more desirable time and space. In this manner we learn to live fourth-dimensionally; and patterns from this dimension are automatically projected on the screen of time and space as three-dimensional experiences and conditions.

What a marvelous thing it is to realize we are not bound by any outer condition! Man possesses the power to imagine goals to be already realized, and to see them come into manifestation with relative ease. All that is required is discipline and a sense of responsibility. We sometimes claim to desire an experience but will not take the responsibility for initiating the creative process. We often expect others to do for us what we ought to do for ourselves, allowing them to be masters of destiny while we remain victims of circumstances or pawns of the superior will of others.

After the Technique, What?

Once you have become skilled in the practice of the technique and have come to the point where you think and feel as though the goal were now reached; what do you do? Sometimes it takes a little time for the desire to unfold as the chosen condition, but it will unfold out of the stuff of which all life experiences are formed. If, after the practice of the technique, you are infused with ideas for constructive action, by all means get into action. The action will not be the cause of the finished result; it will only be the partial effect of the prime *cause;* which is the fulfilled state of consciousness. In other words, do what you feel inspired to do to bring your goal closer; do not merely sit and expect everything to take place around you without your having to lift a finger. But, if you do not know what to do, and cannot see how to begin to get into constructive action, then do nothing outwardly. Rest in the mental state of, "It is already done!" The fulfilled state of consciousness itself will do the rest.

Life is one organic whole, a series of connected parts. This is why states of consciousness, if maintained, have an effect upon our environment. We begin to attract things, circumstances, and people who will be part of our world once we rest in the consciousness of, "It is already done!"

The time it takes for your dream to come into concrete form, after you have used the technique properly, is the time it takes for all of the ingredients to come together according to natural law in this world. I emphasize *properly* in reference to using the technique of creative imagination. If it is not done properly the results will not be forthcoming. *This technique works every time as long as it is practiced properly, and as long as our desire is realistic.*

One who exclaims, "It may work for others but it doesn't work for me!" is admitting his own inability to use it. A natural principle is unfailing; it works every time, and if it works for one person it will work for another person just as readily. There are no special people; there are some who are more able than others, and more aware than others. The steps are: *mental-emotional balance; vivid picturing of the ideal as a realized fact; making it real by mental affirmation and actual feeling it to be so; and then resting until the new state of consciousness becomes permanent.* Our desires must be realistic if we expect to see them fulfilled. For a person, lacking in native ability, to desire an experience which is beyond his capabilities is unwise. Also, we must examine our motives to be sure we are dreaming useful dreams relative to the future. If we are using the technique to manipulate other people, satisfy whims, or gratify immature urges, we are not using it wisely. We should also carefully examine our desires because we are sure to move in the direction of their fulfillment if we harbor them; and it may be that current desires, when fulfilled, will not be satisfactory, or useful to future conditions. With ability comes responsibility.

How often do we need to practice the technique relative to a specific goal? With regularity, until the state of consciousness desired is firmly maintained. Once we are able to live in the state of fulfillment, without wavering, we can dispense with the technique itself. The state of consciousness will insure the fulfillment of the ideal. If we waver, however, then we can use the technique until we are firm in our desired state of consciousness. We know we are settled in this desired state when thoughts, feelings and actions are synchronized in relationship to our chosen goals.

Repeated sessions, if not experienced with total feeling, will be in vain; as are prayers uttered without conviction. There is no magic in the performance of the technique; one proper execution of the process can be sufficient. But do it as often as needed to insure the stable desired state of consciousness.

One may wonder if more than one goal can be worked with at one session. If the goals are interrelated they can be taken as part of the total picture. Or, one can use the technique to *see* and *feel* fulfillment in

the complete life pattern, thus insuring orderly unfoldment in all departments of the pattern and experience.
A consciousness of fulfillment guarantees fulfillment in
all areas of life. It may be, however, that specific areas
need personal attention for it is seldom that a person is
fully aware and open.

One should reflect deeply and carefully before expending energy in the reaching of goals. It is important
that one have a sense of working in harmony with nature and that one really wants to live with what is desired, after it is realized. Many men and women are unhappy because they are living with the effects of their
previous desires. Instead of making needed adjustments,
or instead of using the creative process to form a new
and more desirable life pattern, they bemoan their fate
and elect to live with discontent. Their basic reason for
doing this is a poor self-image; they do not feel they de-
serve anything better. Or, having brought the condition
upon themselves, they live with it as self-punishment.

One cannot wait forever for the evidence of unerring
guidance to manifest in mind and consciousness; a
decision must be made. It is better to try our abilities
and learn to use them creatively than to wait and never
do anything. Decisions, even if unwise (upon retrospec-
tion) afford an opportunity for us to learn by experience. By making wrong decisions we, in time, learn to
make correct ones.

If you need more education in order to function in
the capacity you desire to fill, then seek out information. Read, attend classes, ask advice from experts.
Do not waste time reading books by authors who have
not proven the worth of what they expound. Do not ask
advice from people who are not successful or knowledgeable. Go straight to the point, always. Get the facts and
then put the information to work with constructive action.

It may be that you need to change your pattern of

daily living. Are you wasting time? Are you wasting energy by making useless motions? Are you spending too much time talking, or just hanging around, with people who are not goal-oriented or who are negative thinkers? Do you have short term, and long term, goals for yourself?

What about your quiet conversations with yourself? Are you positive, or negative, as far as mental conversations that go on inside your own mind? What about your verbal conversations with others? Do you speak in a cheerful, optimistic, manner? Do you allow opinions of others to influence you, or their negative moods to cause you to be depressed? We are under no moral obligation to keep company with people who are chronic negative thinkers and thus allow them to poison our minds.

Do you know how to get along with other people? Do they feel better as a result of their contacts with you? We are wise to learn to be appropriate to our social environment and to get along easily with the people with whom we choose to live, and do business. Are you well groomed, well spoken and well mannered? Are you aware of the social rituals which assist smooth relationships between people?

Contentment and Self-Confidence

To be contented does not imply total satisfaction with the way the environment presently appears. But, inner contentment is the firm base from which we work to put our environment in order. Contentment, cheerfulness and self-confidence need not be dependent upon externals at all. Remember, our environment mirrors us or we mirror our environment. If we are to be cause, and not effect, we have to take our stand in consciousness.

First comes self-confidence, then: decisions; creative action; and fulfillment. Remember, our world reflects our state of consciousness. Therefore, be settled in consciousness first. Let thoughts, feelings and actions be in harmony. Everything else will unfold in natural order.

If we are desperate, and try to create an environmental situation to insure peace and contentment, we will never succeed. Something will ever be missing, because we will have made ourselves dependent upon an external condition. Likewise, if we try to attract the right people to us, hoping that the relationships will give us happiness and fulfillment, we are again depending upon externals. We will tend to share with persons who can fulfill our needs, trying to become whole by working out a relationship with individuals who are not whole in themselves.

To be contented and self-confident does not mean that we are entirely self-sufficient, and not in need of harmonious working relationships with others. It means we can enter into mature relationships and not be compelled because of neurotic compulsions.

When we are *ready* in consciousness, we will have the experiences we want in life. When *desire is equal to acceptance* then no reasonable circumstance can be denied us. This is the whole key behind the philosophy of positive thinking; and it is, likewise, the key to effective prayer. When positive thinking results in affirmative feeling and action then the fruitage is evident. When prayer changes from desiring the object of prayer, *to the conviction that it is a present reality,* then prayer is effective.

Faith is the substance of things hoped for, the evidence of things unseen; so the great prophets have stated. To walk by faith is to live in the mental and emotional state that would be ours were our desires now fulfilled, even if sense-perception gives contrary evidence for the time being. Remember, we have said that experience proceeds out of our state of consciousness; therefore, we must be stable in mind and conviction if we are to see our dreams externalized.

It is not uncommon for golf instructors to have their pupils watch a professional in action even before any instruction is given relative to holding the club, proper stance and how to swing. This is for the purpose of allowing the subconscious mind to photograph the picture of the proper procedure, in order to help the student begin correctly and avoid mistakes. Even basketball players who take time to *imagine* themselves making successful shots, when they cannot actually practice, find their skills remain sharp. Salesmen who carry a mental picture of themselves as being successful, tend to be successful. In short, we are able to do well when we can imagine ourselves doing well. *A man becomes what he thinks about because dominant mental pictures mold consciousness and reflect as behavior and experience.*

Every teacher of truth has said it: *whatever reasonable thing a person can mentally conceive, believe to be true, and persist in holding steady in mind, will surely come into expression.*

Healthy seeds planted in fertile soil are sure to sprout and grow after their own kind. Corn comes from corn, beans from beans, potatoes from potatoes. Good fortune follows positive thinking, failure follows negative thinking and unwise behavior. The laws of nature are sure. Like produces like. We can often tell what our past has been by examining our present experiences, and what our future will be by examining our present thoughts and attitudes.

Speaking of Attitudes

How is your present attitude concerning people, places and things? Are people alright the way they are, or are they all in need of being changed? Do you really pray for, and bless, others? Do you wish all people well and desire that they prosper and be in health? Do you think it is alright to take advantage of others? Do you think others can take advantage of you? Are you comfortable in the places you have to function? Can you handle the stuff of this world freely and with understanding?

One of the reasons why some cannot get along with associates is that they are hostile to them, and really do not like them. Or, they feel insecure and must be forever proving themselves to be superior. Remember the key: *we can only experience in our lives that which we can believe to be true of others.* A person may say, "I have practiced positive thinking and the technique of creative imagination according to instructions, but I am still a failure." Then, we ask: "Do you think it is possible for others to fail, be sick, or experience limitations of any kind?" The response will be "yes." Even if we are trying to believe in a constructive manner for ourselves, if we believe in the possibility of limitation for others we are maintaining that belief, or concept, in mind. The law is: mental concepts, or pictures, can externalize as experiences.

Therefore, if we wish others well, and genuinely mean it, we will experience fulfillment. If we even think it is possible for another person to fail at business, get sick, have an accident, or be unhappy in love; we, too, can experience these possibilities. Not because of any law of retribution, but merely because the law is impersonal: that which is within can, and will, manifest without, unless it is modified or neutralized by our taking corrective action in the matter of attitude adjustment.

If we think in terms of taking advantage of others, we ourselves tend to draw a situation in which we are misled and abused. This is why we must ever think in terms of service to others and remember that our success and fulfillment comes through willing channels, with no one being taken advantage of, or suffering, in order that we might prosper. Life fulfills itself through willing and cooperative channels so that everyone is blessed as a result of his participation with us.

Intelligent use of money, tools, food, clothing, and all we handle on a day-to-day basis is essential. We are not slaves to materialism when we pay attention to matters in this world. Attitude is the major factor; we are slaves if we are attached, or if we are not able to function intelligently. Attachment to things, and an aversion to things, are both limitations. Right use of the world's goods is the way of wisdom.

Similarly, acceptance of natural function is the way of wisdom. *It is natural to be in health, to prosper, to appreciate the process of life, and enjoy harmonious relationships with others.* It is not natural to be sick, impoverished, possessed of a negative attitude about life in general, and be in conflict with people. For a person to say, "This world is the place of suffering and tribulation," is ignorance. We work against ourselves when we try to use creative abilities in order to express fulfillment, while at the same time we hold on to negative mental concepts such as: "people are no good," "money is the root of all evil," "its human nature to get sick," "sex is wrong," "you have to get the other fellow before he gets you," and so on and on. Some even harbor the erroneous concept that to be reclusive and out of the mainstream is a "more spiritual" condition.

I have known brilliant and dynamic individuals, heads of far-reaching business organizations, who lived from a state of consciousness which was calm and steady. They knew from experience that expanded consciousness need not interfere with the practical matters of working in the marketplace.

One in business who wants to increase his service, both in quantity and quality, can use creative imagination for specific results. *Daily he should rest in the quiet state, and create in his mind's eye, a scene which would imply the realization of his dreams and ideals.*

Then, as a result of inward change in attitude and consciousness, he will experience a new image of himself and his business. Ideas will flow, energy will be intelligently directed, assistance will be forthcoming, customers will purchase in greater volume and spread the word to others who will, in turn, become links in the success-chain.

We all want to be healthy and to function with ease. If you have a physical problem that needs to be corrected, see to it at once. Perhaps a change in eating habits is in order. Perhaps a more realistic program of exercise. Also, keep in mind the effects of mental attitude and emotions upon the physical body. We differ in our capacities and requirements. What is useful for one person is not necessarily useful for all human beings. There are basic guidelines but individuals will have to adapt the program best suited to themselves.

Health begins in the mind. If we have self-respect and a sound "health consciousness" we are likely to follow through with the routine which best serves our needs. We are wise to avoid self-destructive habits; excessive eating, eating of processed foods, excessive use of tobacco, alcohol, and foods which clog the system. The ideal body weight should be maintained; through a program of exercise, diet, and positive mental attitude. Do not make excuses for being overweight, always tired, or frequently ill. Find the cause of the problem and correct it.

Use the technique of creative imagination to inwardly *see* yourself as healthy, able, and functional in all your parts. Be disciplined in matters of diet. If overweight, put yourself on a program which will supply the body with needed nutritional requirements *and stick to it*! If you respect yourself and have a healthy attitude relative to the world and other people, you will visualize yourself at the proper weight and soon express it. To lose weight it is not necessary to join a weight reduction movement, embark upon a dietary fad, or make the project a major production. Just eat less, eat properly, exercise sufficiently, and *see yourself* with the idealized weight and body form.

The ability to envision circumstances which are not presently in evidence sets man off from all other life forms. Animals live by instinct, they are programmed according to the experiences of their ancestors; altering their patterns only when forced to do so as a result of meeting stress conditions in their environment. They then change their patterns in order to survive. But man has the marvelous ability to image the previously unknown, and then to move into his mental projections. Man can thus be free from routine and compulsive behavior patterns. Man is limited only by natural law, *and by his refusal to imagine states and conditions other than those now perceived.* This imaginative ability is the secret to all progress, all invention, and all modifications in our social structure.

How to Help Others

If you know of other people who need assistance, use the technique of creative imagination for them. First, however, *be sure they want help and be sure you know how to best help them.* Do not meddle, or interfere in the lives of other people. Do not try to change others against their will or interfere with their personal destiny.

First, it is always in order to expect the best of others and to bless them by holding this attitude about them. People usually respond to our unspoken expectations. It has been demonstrated in teaching programs that students perform according to how teachers expect them to perform. Children, especially, respond to the unspoken expectations of parents and teachers. This is also true of adults. Expect, therefore, the best for all you know and meet and, in this manner, call forth their radiant goodness.

If someone has a problem and asks for assistance, do what you can. Perhaps a word of advice, or instruction, is all that is required. Perhaps encouragement and emotional support is needed. You may even be inspired to use the technique of creative imagination on their behalf. If so, proceed as follows.

Go into your quiet place in consciousness. Dismiss any thoughts about the person for whom you will work, relative to claims of limitation. Start from a neutral position. Create in your mind's eye a scene that would imply the freedom required for the person. Bear in mind we do not use telepathy to try to influence the person. *We change our own mind, and consciousness, about the person.* Since the person for whom we work is in our environment, if we see and know only perfection or wholeness, change has to take place. It cannot be otherwise. But, we do not predict how change will come about; nor do we keep looking for signs of change. We do our work and release it. It is done! We do not look back. We do not doubt. *We have treated ourselves, for the other person.*

It is not proper, or ethical, to use superior imaginative abilities to take advantage of other people, or to manipulate them to our advantage. Some people are suggestible and can be so controlled, but it is weakness on our part to take advantage of them. A salesman, for instance, is not to use creative imagination to visualize a specific person buying at a specific time and at a specific price. Instead, the salesman should create the attitude of success within himself and then serve those who are drawn to him, and who are inclined to accept the service.

Can we be influenced by others? Of course; we are forever coming under the spell of urgings sent forth by other people. We can learn to be selective, and not be influenced without conscious consent. And we need not fear negative thoughts or intentions of others who might be misguided enough to send them our way. If there is no belief in the power of negative thinking, there will be nothing in us to which negative thoughts can relate. We will not require prayers for protection, superior will, or any technique or method as defense. All we require is a clear consciousness.

One of the more effective ways to help other people is to set the proper example and to freely share the principles of prosperous living. We can help others according to our capacity, but we should try, by all means, to show people how to help themselves. When we pass our understanding on to others, they too can be self-reliant and independent.

Awakened Consciousness

Bear in mind that as we use creative imagination properly we are not working to condition the subconscious. Some conditioning is inevitable, and the practice will also neutralize negative subconscious conditionings. But our major effort will be to awaken from reliance upon subconscious conditionings so that we function, moment to moment, as self-determined beings; responding to each life situation in an appropriate manner, instead of reacting to a current situation as though it were a similar previous one. A person who is conditioned is compelled to move through life according to his subconscious programming. A person who is aware, and able to analyze properly, is able to function intuitively and spontaneously.

Our environment bears witness to our state of consciousness. Therefore, our major task is to be firm in consciousness; outer events will conform accordingly. It is almost as simple as turning the ignition key and having the motor start in our automobile; we rest in the inner conviction of the experience desired, and the mechanics of nature takes care of the rest of the process.

We should emerge from our session of creative imaginings as one reborn, possessed of a new outlook and a new state of consciousness. If we practice the technique and, afterwards, say, "I hope it works," we have not practiced properly. Living in the new state of consciousness guarantees definite and predictable results.

It is not unusual for a person who uses this process to find that he becomes telepathic and is able to discern the thoughts and intentions of other people. One may even find that precognition, the ability to know the future, begins to develop. This is part of the natural unfoldment process and is nothing to fear, nor to become egotistical about. One also tends to do more soul-searching as a result of learning to function successfully from the inner planes of mind and consciousness; we grow into a greater sense of responsibility, for now that we have creative power, what shall we do with it?

We never force the process. Once we have established the picture of our ideal as being a current reality, in mind and consciousness, we let the pattern unfold in orderly sequence. Stress and strain are not required. The secret is to learn to *dream dreams into reality*. Fond hopes, ideal dreams, and imagined experiences have a way of coming into expression in the three dimensional world. After using the technique, follow guidance as far as creative action is concerned, but do not scheme or use undue persuasion; otherwise, you will interfere with the natural and proper working out of the pattern.

Feel gratitude and thankfulness that your desires are fulfilled and your dreams are realized, even before the evidence is before you. This is confirmation that it is as good as done, for you cannot be thankful for that which does not exist. Gratitude and thankfulness confirms our faith. Do not limit the channels through which your good fortune will flow into expression. Life fulfills

Itself through people; It is the cause of all expression and individuals are but channels. Mind substance is without beginning and without end and can express in various ways throughout eternity. Once the creative flow starts, once you are in harmony with the process, fulfillment will be natural and effortless.

Our security is not in the visible evidence of wealth, but in our concept of self and our conscious relationship with the Life Process. Health, contentment, and prosperity flows from within our own consciousness regardless of external conditions. One who is loving will not lack love. One who is peaceful will never be disturbed. One who is in harmony with nature will never be harmed, even in the midst of confusion or disaster. No matter how others around us express, according to their understanding and consciousness, if we are in tune with life and in harmony with the process of nature, we will never want for any essential thing.

It is better to work in silence and let our creative expression be the evidence of our ability. There is no need to talk openly about goals or make bold claims. Just keep the faith; for faith is the substance of things hoped for, the evidence of things not seen. At times of challenge and seeming delay, do not waver. Then are men tried and tested in the fires of personal self-confrontation. Be steadfast, control your attention, be diligent, be silent, remain in tune with the creative process. Be not afraid. Whatever you are truly led to do, will happen through you if you learn to allow it.

Years ago a certain man retired from business and felt led to spend his time and talents sharing these creative principles, of which we speak, with others. He did not think in terms of "starting small and growing big, in time," he worked from the *end* of his dream. He checked into a fine hotel and spent several days just getting acquainted with the people and the environment. In effect, he made it his home, and he felt comfortable there.

Next, he prepared a lecture series and rented a large hall. Dramatic newspaper advertisements were scheduled and he began his new venture with hundreds of eager students in attendance at his meetings. More came and for years this fine teacher had one of the largest and most influential ministries in his part of the country.

One of the major benefits to be derived from the proper use of the technique of creative imagination is the personal experience of being able to function freely in life. Most barriers are projections of our own mind. Instead of holding mental pictures of limitation, let us see glorious possibilities. Let us dream noble dreams and see them come true.

Remember:

1. The importance of controlled mental imagery.
2. Review the four steps in practicing the technique.
3. Think and feel from the end result.
4. Contentment and self-confidence comes first.
5. Attitude determines life experience.
6. Help others as you have been helped.
7. Feel gratitude and thankfulness from the beginning.
8. Life itself is the source of our prosperity.

Practical Application

1. Read this chapter again and get every step of the process clearly in mind. Then, set aside at least thirty minutes a day for relaxation, thinking and planning, and the use of the technique of creative imagination. If you have no specific goals to work on, use the technique to stabilize your optimistic outlook and positive feelings.

2. If you have been in a rut, or routine, make a conscious effort to change your pattern in order to broaden your perspective, make new contacts, and take the lid off of your imaginative potential. With purpose, move into contact with people, places and things which will force you to communicate in a fresh manner. If need be, make a point of staying away from people who drag you down, and places which weaken your high resolve.

3. Pay attention to your diet. Be sure you are obtaining proper nutrition. Be sure you are getting enough rest, relaxation and exercise.

4. Don't be afraid of change, if change is necessary. To overcome fear; read about successful people; get into action and acquire confidence through doing; read the scripture of your choice; pray and come into an attunement with Life.

*"Think truly, and thy thoughts
shall the world's famine feed;*

*Speak truly, and each word of
thine shall be a fruitful seed;*

*Live truly, and thy life shall be
a great and noble creed."*

"Forgive, and you shall be forgiven."

—*Luke 6:37*

Chapter Four

THE REDEEMING POWER

OF IMAGINATION

One of the most welcome promises given to man is that *creative imagination, properly used, can literally change circumstances and redeem the past.* By adjusting mental concepts through controlled imagination we can undo what has been done as a result of previous unwise thinking. We have only to put the theory to the test to see whether or not it is true.

Let us be reminded that as consciousness we are without name and form. Consciousness is self-existent. I know that I exist. Moods may fluctuate, concepts may change, attitudes may be altered—but I am always aware that I am the observer of these conditions and states. *We do not create a condition or experience, we release it into manifestation through an adjustment of attitude.* All possible human conditions and all possible human experiences are presently available for recognition and manifestation. When we are able to view life from the vantage point of seeing, and accepting, that which we claim we desire for ourselves (or others) we will see the condition emerge on the scene of sense perception. Whether we express prosperity or limitation, health or illness, creativity or lack of ability, depends upon our state of consciousness; which in turn depends upon attitudes, concepts and convictions. Our innate clear consciousness is modified by self-opinion, memories of previous experience, and the concepts we accept from others or arrive at by ourselves.

If my consciousness is the result of attitudes, memories, and concepts then I can alter my state of consciousness by altering attitudes, memories and concepts. We are the center of our environment and the environment revolves around us, from our point of view. We are this moment where we belong according to our present state of consciousness.

The majority of people in this world are victims of past decisions and the memories of previous experiences. Remember, desires tend to fulfill themselves unless they are modified or neutralized. How many desires of the past, long forgotten, still linger in the subconscious mind awaiting the occasion of fruition? How many memories of previous failures, rejections, or painful encounters with life lie buried in the recesses of the subconscious and still modify and temper our behavior and relationships with others? Little does the average person know to what extent he is compelled, or influenced, by the weight of mental-emotional conditionings.

Three Classifications of Subconscious Impressions

Mental impressions are usually recorded on the subconscious level along with all of the emotion and memory of related incidents. That is, we take into the subconscious filing system everything to which the senses are exposed at a given moment. For instance, if a young man is harshly treated on a job situation he will retain the memory of the harsh treatment, along with the memories of the work environment and the other people in that environment. He may dislike even the memory of the environment or the kind of work with which he was involved. Mention of a similar environment, or the meeting of similar psychological types who were in that environment, will evoke feelings of resentment, shame, hate, or whatever is the nature of the person to express. Sometimes when our emotions are restimulated we become unreasonable and make prejudicial statements, experience again some of the emotional pain of the past, and even become confused or depressed.

People are easily confused when their firm concepts are challenged. Because we are not accustomed to remaining objective at all times, we allow ourselves to become anchored by concepts and attitudes and, in this manner, feel somewhat secure. However, when our concepts are challenged and our attitudes altered, we become fearful and unsettled. How often have we heard the expression: "A person has to believe in something!" Believing allows conviction and conviction lends stability. There is a superior way; to move beyond believing to *knowing*. But, let us start at the beginning.

The first classification of subconscious impressions deals with ones we are now allowing into our consciousness. What we accept into mind and feeling-nature now, will modify our lives in the future. This is why we should be aware, selective, and creatively decisive at all times. Learn to monitor the sensory input as you converse with others, listen to the news broadcasts and read newspapers, magazines and books. Learn to discriminate and allow into your mind only that which is "true and of good report." Do not be impressed just because you are addressed in a serious tone of voice, or with emotional impact. Use intelligence and discern the truth, always. Use creative imagination to intentionally adjust attitude and states of consciousness.

The sooner we learn that no external cause is responsible for our experiences in life, the better off we will be. It is easy to blame others, economic policies, lack of education, unfortunate beginnings, and even the planets, for our ups and downs. The simple fact is that we are the product of our own state of consciousness. Present-time mental states are determining current experiences. These mental states may be partially the result of past intentions and accepted concepts, but we need not cling to them. Such mental states can be redeemed as a result of the proper use of creative imagination. If this is not true, then we must be content to remain in bondage forever, or until some external agency comes to our rescue. Our conscious decision and ability to use awakened imagination can save us from misfortune, pain and suffering.

The second classification of subconscious impressions has to do with impressions accepted in the past, which are now bearing fruit. If what is unfolding in our lives is acceptable and in accord with our ideal of what life should be for us, then we can allow the process to continue. If need be, we can alter our mental states and adjust our attitude, and in this way modify the externalization of events.

A major rule is: never become emotionally reactive to any unwanted experience. To do so is to allow ourselves to be the effect of the condition. If we are to be the master of circumstances we must remain objective and in a position of command. If a problem persists, analyze the contents of your mind and consciousness to see what there is in you which relates to it. Why are you accepting it? Why are you allowing it to be a part of your experience? It may be that the present unpleasant situation is the result of a previous mental cause, or even lack of attention to details; then change the mental pattern and take care of the details. It may be that what we are experiencing, as a problem, is not the result of a previous desire but is, instead, the result of our current acceptance of limitation because we have become bored with life, or feel a need to punish ourselves. Handle mental impressions in this second classification, not as past causes, but as current ones—because, even though incurred in the past, they are current impressions. We do not have to actually go into the past to correct causes which were started then; we can handle such causes as currently existing ones, because they *are* currently existing.

The third classification of subconscious impressions deals with deepseated and, therefore, unknown at the present, impressions. They will either become active in due time, or they will be neutralized. It is not necessary for us to become involved in a program of depth self-analysis in order to roam through the corridors of the unconscious. *It has been demonstrated that positive action and success in reaching goals tends to decondition the subconscious negative patterns. We become more able and more sane to the degree that we are functional.*

To blame the past for present misfortune is disaster. If one can easily release past painful or unpleasant memories, so much the better. I did not say we should forget; I suggested *release*. Forgetting is really suppression. What is suppressed in the mind must one day be brought to the surface and confronted. *Release, however, means that we have the memory of past experiences but without the emotional charge attending them. In other words, such memories comprise information which we can use, but without compelling power.*

We are vitally alive to the degree that we can remain on harmonious terms with nature. When toxic waste accumulates in the body, failure patterns dominate our consciousness, painful memories persist, and we no longer have meaning and purpose; we begin to grow old, become ill and move in the direction of physical death. We can be vibrant and creative all the years of our lives if we will but learn to cooperate with nature and work with never-failing principles of mind and consciousness.

Redeeming the Past With Creative Revision

The process of revision is a simple exercise in the use of creative imagination. If you are bothered by a sense of failure, resentments, or feelings of guilt, do this. Become quiet and recall the major cause of the pain or unpleasantness. Relive it, in imagination, *with*

all of the tones of reality as you wish it had happened!
Do this with vivid mental imagery and with strong feel-
ing. You are not changing what happened in time and
space; you are neutralizing the emotional content of
the memory picture. When feeling is discharged from
the mental picture, the compelling power is vanquished.
You will be able to scan the contents of your subconscious mind without emotional reaction. You will find
that you immediately have more energy, greater
powers of concentration and increased enthusiasm.

This is the easiest way to handle negative, or unwanted, subconscious urges. We may never understand
why others treated us unfairly, or why we "didn't get
the breaks," but we *can* remove the pain from the
memory bank. We have to want to do it and be willing
to go through the process if we expect to be free from
the compulsions of the subconscious.

Of course, we need not use the technique of creative
revision if we can, from a mature level of understanding, accept the fact that our past experiences were the
result of our state of consciousness and that no one was
really to blame. Understanding, forgiveness and release can be almost immediate if we are willing to assume a responsible attitude.

On a day-to-day basis, if need be, we can use the
process of creative revision. In the evening, scan the
events of the day and become aware of mistakes made,
or of rejections and failures. Resolve not to duplicate
mistakes and, if necessary, *revise* the episodes of
rejection and failure. By this process we can clear
mind and consciousness on a daily basis and not accu-
mulate destructive and limiting subconscious patterns.
After reviewing the day, revise it in imagination and
relive it as you wish it had been. Then sleep the night
through and awaken refreshed and renewed.

Pay attention to the state of mind you maintain as
you go to sleep, for this is what we take into the subconscious levels. Our pre-sleep states tend to become per-

manent in consciousness, as well as modify our sleeping experience. It is well to spend a few minutes prior to sleep in reading inspirational material or in meditation. We are then not likely to take the stresses of the day into the realm of the subconscious.

We can use the technique of creative revision to rid ourselves of undesirable mental-emotional characteristics we may have been nurturing for years. Or, we can use it along with creative imagination to see ourselves as being free from restricting mental-emotional conditions. We can literally be born again, over and over, into ever more expanded states of consciousness once we determine to take the initiative. We find, through practice, that the journey into consciousness is far more thrilling than any journey we might take in the surface world alone.

Catching the Vision of Possibilities

The only way out of a problem is into the solution. The only way to see dreams come true is to learn to catch the vision of possibilities and become enthused enough, and convinced enough, to really believe. One of the most influential teachers of the positive approach to life is Norman Vincent Peale. But, let him tell the story that had a bearing on his life when he was a young man:

"Many years ago in a church of which I was pastor, an old man taught me a lesson I have never forgotten. He was a wonderful person. He never went beyond the third grade in school, so he had insight which he might have lost if he had carried his education higher. He just had natural sagacity—the ability to penetrate things from outside in, from underneath up, and down from the top.

"He lived up in the David Harum country in New York State. He was the personification of old David Harum himself. Wherever he put out his hand, money just sprang into it. He had a marvelous alchemy in his touch.

"When I went to this church, I found that they had a $55,000 debt. They all told me there was no money with which to pay it off, although this was back in 1928. Listening to some of the negative thinkers, I got the impression that they loved this debt, that they wouldn't lose it for the world, that they would be homesick without it. But finally we had a meeting, and after much discussion the most amazing resolution was passed. It said, in effect, 'We are sure we can't do this, but we ought to make some kind of gesture. Therefore be it resolved, knowing that we can't do it, that we will try to raise—not the whole amount—but $20,000.'

" 'Now,' they said to me, 'you had better go out and talk to Brother Andrews.'

"I did, the next day. He lived out in the country in a little old-fashioned house on a hillside. I rapped on the door, and he opened it. He always wore his glasses far down on his nose. They were those half-moon kind that you seldom see any more.

"I said, 'How are you, Brother Andrews?'

"He said, 'Come in.'

"When we were in the old-fashioned parlor, I said to him, 'We had a meeting of the Official Board last night.'

" 'I heard you did.'

" 'I thought I'd come out and have a talk with you.' 'I thought you would,' he said. 'What's on your mind?'

"I said, 'Well, we're hoping to raise some money.'

" 'How much are you going to raise?'

" 'Twenty thousand dollars.'

" 'M'mm, is that so? Well, all right. Speak up. How much do you want?'

" 'I just wondered how much you are going to give.'

" 'Oh, the answer to that is easy. Not a nickel. Not a cent. Now that that's settled, what else do you want to talk about?'

"I said, 'I guess there isn't anything else to talk about.'

"He looked at me for a minute. Then he said, 'I won't give you any money, but I'll tell you what I will do. I'll pray with you.'

"That didn't fill me with any burning enthusiasm. It wasn't prayer I was after. It was cold, hard cash. Furthermore, I didn't think prayer would get me anywhere when it came to raising money. I had been taught not to pray for material things. But I agreed.

" 'Get down on your knees,' said Brother Andrews.

"His carpets were thin, too, I will tell you. But this old man evidently knew the Lord pretty well, because he talked to Him in a very free and easy manner.

"This was his prayer: 'Lord, here we are. We have to raise some money. This young minister is a nice fellow, but, Lord, he doesn't know much! He's the biggest will-nilly I ever met in my life. Why, Lord, he doesn't know the first thing about business or how to do something big. He has little faith. He doesn't believe in himself, or in the ministry. Now, Lord, if he is only going to try to raise $20,000 I won't give him a nickel. But if he will believe he can raise the whole $55,000, I will give him $5,000. Amen.'

"We got off our knees, and I was pretty excited. I said to Brother Andrews, 'Where are we going to get the rest of it?'

"He said, 'Where you just got the first $5,000. You prayed for it and you got it, didn't you? Now, do you want to know where to get the rest?'

" 'Yes,' I said, in some bewilderment.

"He said, 'Get down on your knees again.'

"He got me down on my knees again. Then we put a plain white card on the table. 'Lord,' he said, 'we want to know where to get the rest of the money. Give me a name, O Lord.'

"There was a silence. Then he said, 'I have it!' I

guess he had it all the time, but he was giving credit to the Lord, and actually it was the Lord, working through him.

"He said, 'I am going to write down the name of Dr. So-and-so. He will tell you he hasn't got any money, but I am on the Finance Committee at the bank, and I know exactly what he has. It says in the Bible that if you have faith even as a grain of mustard seed, nothing is impossible for you, and I have faith, and I'm going to write him down for $5,000. Amen.'

"He stood up and said to me, 'Now go downtown and get it!'

"I had little confidence in the whole thing, but I drove downtown. When I came to the building where the doctor had his offices, I drove around praying I wouldn't find a place to park, I found one at once.

" 'Well,' I said to the doctor, 'we are raising money.'

" 'I heard you were. Now I suppose you want some from me.'

" 'That's right.'

" 'Well, suppose you tell me how much you think I ought to give.'

"I looked at him and said to myself, 'I wonder if he's good for $500. Maybe I could ask him for a thousand.' Then I remembered Brother Andrews' face with faith all over it. I took a deep breath, and said, 'Dr. So-and-so, I am going to give you the privilege of giving us $5,000.'

"He said, 'Five thousand dollars! That's `a tremendous amount of money!'

"I said, 'It sure is.'

"Well, he mumbled in his beard for a minute. Then he said, 'I think it's preposterous. But something comes over me as I'm standing here. I'll give you the $5,000.'

"I didn't even say good-bye to him. I jumped into my car, drove back to Brother Andrews' house, screeched up to the door, I burst in on him. 'He did it! He did it!' I cried.

" 'Why, sure he did,' said Brother Andrews.

"I stared at him. 'How did you know?'

"He said, 'Listen, son, I sat here all the time you were driving downtown, not believing he would do it, and I just sent a thought hovering over you all the way down there that he *would* do it, and my thought hit him right between the eyes.'

"I said, 'You know, I saw it hit him!'

"He said, 'It penetrated his brain and it changed his thinking.' Then he shoved me back against the wall and held me with a hand on either shoulder. 'Listen, son,' he said. 'I don't care whether they raised that debt or not. A little old debt is good for the church. I'm investing that $5,000 in you, to try and make a man of faith out of you. A long while ago I discovered an antidote for failure, and it's this. You're never defeated by anything until in your mind you accept the thought that you are defeated. It may have cost me $5,000, but by George, if I've got that idea into your head, it's worth it!' "[*]

This was a personal experience of Dr. Peale's and demonstrates the influence of faith and imagination. Of course, we suggest that one not use such ability for specific happenings but there is no doubt but that the principle works when used by a person of understanding.

Affirmation—Another Useful Tool

The use of affirmations, on the mental or verbal level, is well known to thousands of goal oriented men and women. It is well, therefore, to know the proper way to use them. We have discussed the importance of positive thinking and positive speaking. An affirmation is the result of a purposeful effort to synchronize thought, speech and feeling in order to produce definite

Norman Vincent Peale, Minister to Millions, Prentice-Hall, 1958; by Arthur Gordon.

effects. The methods we use are for the purpose of altering mental states and adjusting attitudes, for mental states and stable attitudes determine our state of consciousness; and out of consciousness flows our life experience.

An affirmation, used properly, is not a drill used to condition the mind; it is a technique which gives us conscious control over thought and attitude. We select a phrase which embodies our ideal; *again, working from the end of the idealized condition.* When we synchronize our thoughts, words and feelings we become magnetized and our power of concentration is focused on specific targets, or goals. For instance, we might use the following affirmation to realize health and vital function: "I am now in full possession of my natural powers. I am radiant, alive and functional in all my parts. Mind, emotional nature, and physical body, function together harmoniously and properly in all ways."

For prosperity: "I am now serving life in my proper capacity. Therefore, consciousness fulfills itself in my personal life as the things, circumstances, and associates I require for unrestricted expression." Note that money itself is not the sole symbol of prosperity; to be prosperous is to have a free flow of needed things, right circumstances and cooperative people.

For personal awakening and unfoldment: "My real nature is pure consciousness. I am the observer as well as the participant in the life process. I am in full command of my mental states, attitudes and states of consciousness at all times. I work in harmony with the Grand Intelligence which controls and regulates the cosmos."

These are but suggestions, one can make up his own affirmation and use it with feeling and inward realization. The secret to success in the use of affirmations is; *dwell upon the essence of the affirmation and, as a result of awakened intuition and the use of discernment, realize the truth embodied therein.*

Affirmations can be used as mental drills, to recondition the subconscious, and to pacify the mind. But the higher benefits will be derived only if one contemplates the *essence* of the affirmation and then awakens to the realization that it is true.

Sometimes there is a conflict between conscious and subconscious levels of mind. One may use an affirmation with positive intent, yet find that subconscious patterns are so firmly entrenched that they cannot be easily neutralized. In this case we then use *persuasion*. The subconscious may resist a direct command, but we will invariably have success if we coax it to change for the better. Concepts are often deeply rooted because they have *survival value* to us. We have found them useful, even if restricting. One may, for instance, have partial peace of mind by believing in even an unreasonable philosophy of life. Unreasonable concepts equal peace of mind, therefore, survival and a degree of contentment. Of course, this is the "ignorance is bliss" state of consciousness. An affirmation of a persuasive nature for health might be: "I now by gradual degrees, release the patterns and concepts which have stood in the way of expressing perfect physical health. I now accept new attitudes and realizations which will reflect as perfect health on all levels." We are to *encourage* change for the better instead of demanding it.

Group participation in affirmations can be useful in inspiring and motivating the individuals who will enter into the practice. The "rah, rah, rah" type of affirmation may stir feelings, but the results will not be as lasting as *affirmation used consciously to increase realization and bring about a permanent adjustment in mental attitude.*

Reinforce the Feeling of Accomplishment

Unless one is powerfully motivated and possessed

of deep inner convictions, evidence of progress must be forthcoming as reinforcement to the mind and emotional nature. When we are rewarded for effort expended we tend to be more enthusiastic and to anticipate the future with confidence. This is why short-term goals are needed, because results are almost immediate. This builds a success-pattern in mind and consciousness and prepares for greater success. Also, the positive feelings resulting from accomplishment neutralize any subconscious failure impressions. We become healthier, happier and more zestful when we win the games of setting and reaching goals. We become despondent and confused when we fail to win. We lose hope when the future is obscure, and when hope is lost just about all is lost. Until hope can be restored.

No matter how dark the night, or how deep the personal despair: with self-confidence; attunement with the Universal Power; and the proper use of creative imagination—any person can see unfolded from within his own consciousness the true light and glory of the soul redeemed.

Remember:

1. **Creative imagination, properly used, can alter circumstances and redeem the past.**
2. **Learn to handle subconscious impressions.**
3. **Use creative revision intelligently.**
4. **Be a possibility thinker.**
5. **Use affirmations properly for altering states of consciousness.**
6. **Never lose hope!**

Practical Application

1. Read this chapter again and get insight into the subject. Understand especially the three classifications of subconscious impressions. Just by thinking in this direction you may experience a restimulation of suppressed memories, with the attending trauma. Be objective and handle whatever comes up with relative ease. The pain associated with past rejections and failures shuts down our awareness and reduces the flow of available energy through the body. Release of trauma results in an increase in awareness and more energy to be used creatively. Whenever you tend to become bogged down by memories, and pain associated with such memories, bring your attention into present-time awareness. That is, instead of "living in the past," turn your attention to *here* and *now*. Get into communication with your present environment: touch something; look at it; feel it; examine it closely. Touch another person, feel their reality, communicate about the present. This simple procedure will bring you from the past to the present; it will also bring you back from the "future" if you are daydreaming about the future and have gotten stuck there. When we practice the technique of creative imagination we do not have to concern ourselves with moving into future-time, because we always remain **here** and bring the future to *here* and *now*, and *live in it in the here and now*. So, there is no possibility of our being "spaced out," or walking around in a mental fog.

2. Be a *possibility thinker*; examine the possibilities before you at any given time and select the ones which seem most useful. This is sometimes referred to as "brain storming" as it is a time when we allow ourselves to extend our thought processes beyond conditioned limits.

3. Understand well the use of affirmations. If you use

affirmations, use them properly. Do not mumble confused incantations or try to use auto-suggestions. All of the methods prescribed here are for the purpose of awakening awareness, instead of conditioning the mind. Do not play games and pretend to be involved with witchcraft or black magic. Really, any cause we set into motion to produce a specific effect is a magical act; but we need not use words which give the wrong impression to what we are doing.

4. Create an environment for yourself which will support your feelings relative to your desired life style. If you are thinking prosperity thoughts then live in clean, harmoniously decorated surroundings. Dress in comfortable well tailored clothes. Taste is more important than a lot of money so do not plead poverty as an excuse to live an undisciplined and inappropriate life.

NOTES

"Build thee more stately man-
sions, O my soul,
As the swift seasons roll!
Leave thy low-vaulted past!
Let each new temple, nobler
than the last,
Shut thee from heaven with a
dome more vast
Till thou at length art free,
Leaving thine outgrown shell by
life's unresting sea."

"Distinguish therefore states from Individuals in those
States. States change but Individual Identities never
change nor cease. . . ."

—William Blake

Chapter Five

RESTING AT THE SEAT OF POWER

The seat of power, creativity and intelligence is pure consciousness. Out of the pure state of consciousness everything else emerges. Therefore, consciousness is the cause and the support of external manifestation. If a person can learn to consciously rest at the seat of power, creativity and intelligence he can then move onto the field of action with understanding and virtually unlimited potential. The process by which one does this is known as meditation.

When I speak of meditation I do not even suggest, or imply, a mysterious or complicated process. The practice of the methods explained here will not in any way interfere with one's religious beliefs or philosophical views. We are concerned only with bringing ourselves to the true source within, from which everything else is extended into expression.

During our practice of meditation, which takes but a few minutes a day, we are not actively concerned with projects, goals, personal improvement or any dramatic happening. After we learn to meditate we will find that projects are more easily completed, goals are more easily reached, personal improvement is noted, and some unusual and welcome happenings occur; not during meditation, but afterward as a result of our increased awareness and improved ability to function.

Meditation, when properly practiced, is not subconscious conditioning. It differs from the active process of creative imagination. If one desires to use the technique of creative imagination it should be used after meditation, because then the mind will be clear and powers of concentration greater.

Here is how to practice for greatest benefits. Twice a day make an appointment with yourself and retire to a quiet place where you will not be disturbed. This can be any room at home, an unused office at your place of business, or wherever you decide. Just sit upright in a relaxed posture, with hands on your thighs. Close your eyes and become aware of the internal workings of your body. Withdraw attention from feet, legs, hands and arms; bring the *attention* and *feeling* back to the spinal column. Do not use suggestion or effort. Just turn within easily and naturally. Withdraw your attention from the senses so you are no longer aware of your immediate environment. It does not matter if you continue to hear noises at a distance, as long as the greater part of your attention is centered within. Then, lift the *attention* and *feeling* up through the spinal passageway to the midbrain. Do not visualize or use great effort. Flow the attention inwards. *Listen, look, be aware.* If you hear a sound, perhaps a high pitched sound, put your attention on it. Do not analyze, picture, or strain. Just *flow* to the sound. Lacking the perception of a sound just *listen, look and be aware.* Rest in this relaxed, aware condition for several minutes. Do not force it.

With practice you will be able to enter into a serene, clear state of awareness. You will transcend thought, mental images and feelings. Yet, you will be conscious and at peace within yourself. This is not a trance condition, for you will be clear and in full possession of your innate abilities. Do not make the mistake, while meditating, of trying to "see things" or receive solutions to problems. *Meditation is for the purpose of helping us rest at the seat of power, creativity and intelligence.*

After meditation, when we begin to flow our attention outward through the senses, we can retain the clear awareness and function from a more objective and capable point of view. Come out of meditation easily and feel high-frequency energies flowing down from the brain, through the nervous system, into the body. Feel that all systems: circulatory; lymphatic; and glandular, are functioning perfectly. Just assume this to be so. Feel at peace and in harmony with your environment.

Now, if you feel inclined, this is the time to use creative imagination for the positive purposes already decided upon. Many find that it is not required at this time, because they are so aware, and so intuitive and spontaneous, they just seem to do the right things at the right time and all relationships are in perfect harmony. Goal setting, problem solving and decision making are best gone into at this time, just after meditation. One of the reasons for this is that we are then mentally and emotionally unburdened and can make more rational decisions.

There are other benefits to be derived from regular and proper meditation practice. Tension is one of the major enemies of people in an industrial society. Meditation allows deep relaxation and removes tension. The result is better function on the mental, emotional and physical levels and even a clearing away of some psychosomatic illnesses. Through self-understanding, as a result of meditation, we become more honest with ourselves and more realistic in our relationships. We tend to think in terms of essentials and we use time and energy more wisely.

Meditators commonly report an increase in their powers of concentration, better memory, more energy and a more optimistic outlook toward life. Also, because of greater self-sufficiency meditators do not rely as much on drugs, alcohol, overeating, or neurotic social games.

It is important to meditate on a regular basis. Ten or fifteen minutes twice a day is a useful pattern for the average person. This keeps a person anchored in pure consciousness and helps him retain a balanced outlook. Improved function, and performance, will be the indicators of success in meditation practice. Be alert, at times of great challenge, and avoid using meditation as an occasion to escape from responsibilities. Preoccupation with occult matters is a diversion from the personal responsibility of functioning in this world. Since we are concerned with learning how to function creatively, out of our true center which is consciousness, it is really a practical step to learn to meditate effectively.

Remember:

1. **The seat of power, creativity and intelligence is pure consciousness.**
2. **Make an appointment daily to meditate.**
3. **Turn naturally to the inward source, rest, and then flow outward.**
4. **After meditation, relate intelligently with your environment.**

Practical Application

1. Because this title is distributed to the mass market and written primarily for the purpose of encouraging the reader to come to terms with goals and human relationships, this chapter on meditation was purposely kept short. For the person whose main desire is more effective functioning in the social mainstream, meditation as suggested herein will be most effective. For readers who desire to study the meditation process more in depth, we suggest our title, *This Is Reality*, which can be obtained from us, or through your distributor.

2. Meditation is not difficult, dangerous or impractical. All one has to do is meditate as recommended, for a period of several weeks, and the positive results will be noted without fail. Do not, while meditating, look for phenomena or psychic escape (such as trance, etc.). Always be *here* and *now* and be the witness as the mind calms down and the feeling nature becomes clear. Just sit in the "I am the conscious witness" experience. Being objective gives us great control over mental processes, feelings and relationships because we learn to function wisely and not out of emotional need.

NOTES

NOTES

"If therefore ye are intent upon wisdom a lamp will not be wanting and a shepherd will not fail, and a fountain will not dry up."

— *Anonymous*

"You see, Life is intelligent. Life is all-powerful. And Life is always and everywhere seeking expression. What is more, it is never satisfied. It is constantly seeking greater and fuller expression. The moment a tree stops growing, that moment the life in it starts seeking elsewhere for means to better express itself. The moment you stop expressing more and more of Life, that moment Life starts looking around for other and better outlets."

— *The Law of the Higher Potential*
Robert Collier

Chapter Six

DRAWING UPON THE ENDLESS SOURCE

Have you ever had the experience of relaxing, or of performing a routine task which did not call for conscious attention, and noticed ideas and creative projects taking form in your mind? These patterns well up from the depths of the subconscious level of mind as a result of our urge to express in new and often novel ways.

The subconscious level of mind contains billions of bits and pieces of data which have been filed away over the years; the natural creative process assembles them and we are then able to project unique plans and patterns into the outer world. As unlimited as the supply of data in the subconscious may seem to be, there is a limit to it because the information recorded at this level is limited to what we have previously accepted and stored. But, there is an unlimited source of information and power. This source is universal mind. We are in tune with universal mind through the subscious level of our own mind because human mind is an individualization of universal mind. Whatever data is stored in universal mind is available to us. And, more than this, *the evolutionary energy of the universe is available to us once we learn to open ourselves to the flow.*

The First Step in the Process

The first step is to be willing to be open to the flow of

creative ideas and to assume that guidance can come from within in a practical and realistic manner. Be reminded that the process works best when we are relaxed and free from tension. Conscious mind effort and anxiety will interfere with the natural flow of ideas. This is why most useful creative ideas come at random moments, when we are relaxed, and not when we are at the desk trying frantically to force the process.

For guidance. Let us assume you need guidance in making a major move, or in solving a problem. Relax and *confront* the problem. That is, recognize it and accept the fact that you need inspiration, more information, or perhaps even keen insight. Assemble all the known factors in your mind's eye and *assume* that the guidance will be forthcoming. Then, either rest quietly in a waiting attitude or occupy yourself with routine activities. Perhaps a change of pace just to get your conscious mind off the problem. Water the lawn, take a walk, watch television, go out to dinner, read an interesting book just for relaxation and diversion. Before long you will become aware of ideas, possible solutions, and insights bubbling to the surface of your mind. You can then select the most logical among those offered, or the ones which *feel* right.

For planning your day. The night before, meditate awhile and then, while in a relaxed after-meditation mood, turn your attention to the day ahead. Review your projects, think about your schedule, and let it all take shape before your inner vision. New ideas will come, jot them down while they are clear in your mind. The next morning scan your appointment book and go forth with enthusiasm and concentration, and fully synchronized; mentally, emotionally and physically.

A question comes: "How does one tell the difference between intuitive guidance and wishful thinking?" With practice there will be a feeling of *rightness* when an intuitive thought comes. When in doubt, *and if there is everything to gain and nothing to lose by checking it out in Immediate application,* act upon the urge and see what happens. With practice you will learn to recognize intuitive guidance and ignore wishful thinking.

When we are in balance we are spontaneous and decisive. Our timing is perfect. We just seem to do the right things at the right time, say the right words, and work in harmony with everything that goes on about us. When the thought comes to call a friend or associate for no particular reason, call right away—*for no particular reason.* Do not try to make anything out of it, just call and say hello. It may be important that you call, or it may be that your thoughts crossed in the mental spaces. Either way, communication is always worthwhile.

Remain Open and in Contact

Water cannot flow through a blocked pipeline. Life force cannot flow through a blocked, or severely damaged, nerve. Thoughts cannot flow through a distorted mind. Creative intelligence cannot function through a clouded human consciousness. Human relations cannot flourish without contact and with no flow back and forth. *To be prosperous and to be in health we have to be open to the world within and to the world without.* When we are open and the lines of communication are clear life can fulfill itself through us.

Meditation, self-analysis and the use of creative imagination keeps us in free communication with the inner dimensions. Willingness to confront life, reasonable goals to work for, and a mature attitude and relationship with people assures communication with the world without.

Sometimes the pressure of work results in a decrease in energy, interest and willingness to face life. When this happens it usually means that we have allowed our lines of communication to become partially jammed: either with incorrect data; lack of planning (and follow-through); frustration due to uncompleted projects; or concern over whether or not our goals are worthwhile.

We then have to evaluate the situation and take corrective action before we sink into apathy and lose hope altogether. The first step is to back off a little bit and examine conditions from an objective point of view.

1. *Data, or information at hand.* To function intelligently we need facts relative to a situation. We have to be able to think clearly and plan in a reasonable manner. If you do not have the facts relative to a project, then acquire them. If something is not clear, seek clarification.

2. *Planning wisely and well.* If your facts are accurate, relative to a project, then go over your plans. Are they logical? Have you used the creative process properly, working from the *end* of the project? Are the people involved the right people for the roles they are to play? Is the project worthwhile and altogether useful? Have you been doing your part? Are you letting matters unfold, or are you pushing and manipulating?

3. *Frustration.* Sometimes, when a project takes more time to materialize than previously expected, we grow impatient and become frustrated. Again, step back and be objective. Perhaps the project was initiated in haste? Perhaps some factors need to be modified? Once the process is rolling and matters are pretty much automatic perhaps you should be thinking of new projects while the current one fulfills itself in due time? It may be that you are experiencing a temporary down-cycle because of some minor rejection, physical illness, poor nutrition or regular mood-energy changes we all go through. Even healthy, well nourished, men and women experience highs and lows on a regular basis. This is a natural built-in biological rhythm peculiar to all living things. Sometimes, then, nothing is wrong with you or your project; all you have to do is let the mood pass.

Frustration can also be a sign of confusion of information, impatience and too many challenges being thrown at us at the same time. This is a good time to get away for a few minutes, or hours, to become collected and objective before handling matters. Once on top of the situation we can handle it. Sometimes a complete change of pace is useful: taking a drive, an outing with friends or family, a round of golf, or a walk alone. When walking alone let the mind roam free, the muscles be relaxed, and *observe the environment.* This will bring you back into attunement and help to arrange thoughts and feelings into a more balanced perspective.

4. *The value of our goals.* We sometimes entertain doubts regarding the value of our selected goals, even after we have moved in the direction of reaching them. It will not hurt if we modify our plans or even change our goals once we have come to a more mature level of understanding. More often, however, doubts about the value of goals already set are due to premature planning. We should learn to avoid acting on emotional impulse. Enthusiasm is one thing; emotionalism is something else. Try to be sure about the value of your goals before expending energy in their fulfillment.

Guidelines for the Selection of Goals and Projects

How often do we hear the complaint: "I just don't know what to do with my life!" Many people wander through the corridors of time in aimless confusion. I have talked with men who, in the eyes of their friends and associates, had achieved a high level of success who told me, "I wonder, sometimes, if it has been worthwhile? Something still seems to be missing." Or, persons trying to break away from a routine job situation in order to move into a field where initiative and challenge will bring out their creative best, do not know where to begin. There are, too, men and women who have had their lives changed by circumstances and who must "begin again" to make a new life.

What we do depends upon our *native ability, desire to render service,* and *talent in using the basic creative tools* which will result in success in all our ventures. When each person is doing the thing he can best do to contribute to the welfare of mankind, and to the planet itself, then harmony prevails and all living things prosper.

Some people, who are brutally materialistic, live by the philosophy: "This world is a jungle and it is a matter of the survival of the fittest!" Such people think in terms of surviving at all costs, even at the expense of other people and the planet itself. They exploit, use and destroy, if need be, to reach their goals. This book is not for them, unless they change their state of consciousness and their motives.

Most people want to do the right thing and truly desire to be of service. *What is real service? When we render the most useful contribution we can to the welfare of the human race, all life forms and the evolution of the planet.* We are not endowed with the same abilities, inclinations or capacities to function. The important thing is for each of us to find where we can best function and there unfold our true potential. We need educators, scientists, business administrators, doctors, nurses, architects, builders, manufacturers, distributors, store owners, sales representatives, artists, writers, and people in all useful capacities. We need people to make us laugh and to make us thoughtful, to make us extend ourselves and to give us emotional support at times. We are all necessary in the grand scheme. *The secret of personal fulfillment is to work in harmony with the total process.*

Do not think merely in terms of making money, becoming famous, or of gratifying childhood fantasies. To be compensated for service rendered, to be recognized, to fulfill some subconscious needs—is not out of line, or wrong. But let not these motives be the driving motives. Think in terms of service, in both quality and quantity.

Be sure you are living your own life. Are you doing what you are, because you want to? Or are you doing it because you think you must, or because you are fulfilling the ideals of someone else: a parent; teacher; or friend? You may be living out someone else's dreams and not fulfilling your personal destiny at all. Centuries ago, a wise man told his disciple: "It is better to try to fulfill your own destiny and fail in the attempt, than to imitate the life pattern of another and be successful in that venture." No one really wants to go through life being an imitation of someone else. No one, who is reasonably intelligent, wants to be in a zombie like trance, apathetic and unresponsive. Millions of people, however, believing themselves to be caught in a web of circumstances: remain the effects of external causes; function in a dream-like condition; and ward off despondency by believing in unreasonable philosophical doctrines. They have not the courage to think, or to act.

If you require courage: pray; read inspirational and motivational books and articles; associate with self-confident people; and try your creative talents in minor directions and projects to acquire skill and a sense of accomplishment. Be bold, but do not be unreasonable. Plan with courageous imagination, but be practical.

If you are religious, or philosophical, and feel you are working in harmony with a Grand Design (which you are when you are in your right place in the cosmic scheme), be sure to do your part and use your abilities fully. Do not blame God if your personal plans do not work out as you originally planned.

Beware of promoters who want you to "come in on a good thing" but who have no money of their own to invest, and of business "opportunities" which are just a little too infallible. Avoid the sales positions where you will be selling a product which is not essential to the health, happiness and welfare of the customer but will return you a profit; this is not real service.

Goals and projects do not always have to do with a life style other than now being experienced. You may already be in your right place and need only to learn how better to function in it. Use the same principles and procedures you would use for new projects to improve upon your present pattern. And, above all, *learn to love the work you do*. Whatever you do, because it is right for you, it is your duty, your place in life; do it with full attention and enjoy the doing of it. Be happy at the task at hand and this will insure that you never fall into the mental trap of believing that happiness and fulfillment will be yours, *sometime*. Now-time is the only moment to be perceived and appreciated.

It is well to be able to live with memories of the past and to plan intelligently for the future, but we must also be sure we are living fully in the present. To move into present-time awareness is to step free of psychosomatic illnesses, regrets, guilt and bitterness. It is to put an end to stress and anxiety. It is to increase awareness, energy, and creativity automatically.

A Never Failing Source

We have said that energy is eternal. It is without beginning and without end; it merely changes form. There is no end to energy because it flows from pure consciousness and forever expresses. There is no end to ideas because ideas take form according to the urging of life, through the mind, to express. We, therefore, have access to a never failing source of supply. But, this supply of resources, things to use, ideas, and creative potential *flows from within us out into the world. Do not make the mistake of assuming that these things are outside of yourself.* Never give in to the feeling of lack or limitation because of a temporary absence of money, things or ideas. You are never alone and never without any needed thing. During times of seeming lack, enter more deeply into your own consciousness and tap the true source of all supply, then you will see the flow begin to manifest as external energy-forms according to your desire and in line with your present need.

That which we are seeking is seeking us; because it is the nature of life to fulfill itself through its own expressions. You and I were born for a purpose; to be channels through which the evolutionary energy can express. Once we learn to attune ourselves to the primal cause and cooperate with it, we will know success beyond our fondest dreams. *The same consciousness which produced the worlds out of itself is individualized as us; so that the worlds might be modified through us to fulfill the perfect pattern maintained from the beginning of time.*

The worlds were produced initially, and ever since, nature has been but making modifications. In our creative acts we do not really create anything; that is, we do not manifacture anew. *We merely rearrange the available material in line with controlled states of consciousness.* Success, however defined, and all of the signs of health and prosperity are not created, but *unveiled.*

We unveil beauty, harmony, health, prosperity, genius and whatever we feel led to bring forth, by making adjustments in attitude, thinking and states of consciousness. At the core of every problem lies the solution. In the correctly stated question lies the answer. Beneath the appearance of discord is the ideal pattern of order and harmony awaiting only our recognition.

Can you "call forth the things that are not (to the senses), as though they were?" If so, you are able to recognize that which needs to be awakened and raised from the dead. No reasonable thing is impossible to you once you learn to see through sense-appearances and recognize the true essence of a situation. Miracles are performed by those who recognize natural, but subtle, laws of nature. What is easy for one who possesses awareness and awakened imagination is impossible for a person who cannot discern. To see truly is to be awake; not to see truly is to be asleep even while *seemingly* awake to the world.

One is asleep to the truth about life when sense-bound and restricted by traditional concepts and opinions of limitation. Such people are referred to, by philosophers, as conscious dreamers. Such dreamers are dreaming the mortal dream; believing themselves to be at the mercy of inherited tendencies and the convictions of the human race. Yet, there is no law which compels us to remain in bondage. There is no outside influence causing us to be contained by the senses. This is why the conscious and deliberate practice of the technique of creative imagination is so useful; it affords us the opportunity to slip free of all restrictions and experience, in thought and feeling, endless possibilities. We refer now to deliberate practice, not to daydreaming and escapism. The latter habit gives temporary relief from pressing circumstances; the former changes consciousness and results in self-transformation.

Practice going to sleep at night with the attitude of wanting to become conscious during your dream experiences. In time you will be aware that you are dreaming; and be a participant, an observer, or a dream "editor" with the ability to alter your dreams at will. Upon awakening you can compare the experience to your normal waking state and see the similarity. This is one of the methods taught by consciousness-expansion teachers to encourage an awakening from the mortal dream state in which most people live.

Remember:

1. We are in tune with universal mind through our own mind.
2. Use the techniques to receive guidance.
3. When you have everything to gain, and nothing to lose, act on intuitive urges immediately.
4. Remain in contact with the worlds within, and without.
5. Be objective and examine yourself and your motives.
6. Think in terms of rendering genuine service.
7. Live your own life; not someone else's.
8. Learn to love the work you do.
9. Be attuned to the never failing source.
10. Learn to be fully awake and perceptive.

Practical Application

1. If you have been reading this book over a period of several days, or weeks (if you have come back to it) return to the list of questions at the end of Chapter Two, and without looking at your previous answers, run through the list again.

2. Practice sitting for daily inspiration and guidance. Many people, in all walks of life, have found it useful to set aside a period of time each day for "thinking and planning" and for being open. If you think you do not have time to give to these creative processes think about the time you perhaps waste in: idle talk; useless motion; television; reading for diversion; too many hours in bed; too long at the dining table; or because you lack organization of time. Time and energy are two things we should use wisely. Also, if you expend energy and use time to make money, how do you spend your money? The way you spend money is the way you spend your life; because if you expend your life for money, it becomes congealed energy which you ought to use wisely.

3. Try planning your days and weeks ahead of time, allowing room for change and modification. Write down your appointments and schedule your time and energy. See how much more you accomplish and how much more free time you have for other creative activities.

NOTES

"Happy is the man that findeth wisdom,
And the man that getteth understanding.
For the gaining of it is better than the
*   gaining of silver.*
And the profit thereof than fine gold.
She is more precious than rubies:
And none of the things thou canst desire
*   are to be compared with her.*
Length of days is in her right hand:
In her left hand are riches and honor.
Her ways are the ways of pleasantness,
And all her paths are peace.
She is a tree of life to them that lay
*   hold upon her.*
And happy is every one that retaineth her."

—Proverbs

"Here is the prime condition of success, the great se-
cret: Concentrate your energy, thought, and capital
exclusively upon the business in which you are
engaged. Having begun on one line, resolve to fight it
out on that line, to lead in it, adopt every improvement,
have the best machinery, and know the most about it.
Finally, do not be impatient, for as Emerson says, 'No
one can cheat you out of ultimate success but your-
self.' "

—Andrew Carnegie

Chapter Seven

SUCCESS UNLIMITED

To be *successful* means to realize a favorable termination of consciously planned projects, and to be such an open channel that life fulfills itself through you without restriction. To be a conscious and willing participant in the life process is to be successful. Success is not measured in terms of money accumulated, prestige acquired, or temporary influence over others. We cannot measure real success by symbols and signs which are, by their nature, temporary.

We are not saying that money is not useful. It is, for it enables us to accomplish much which is of value. Prestige and influence are also useful, if properly handled. But there is a firm base upon which real and permanent success rests. I speak of conscious attunement with the Life Process, and the wisdom gained as a result of years of deep and purposeful study of the principles by which the universe runs.

It is useful to learn to function in this world, because if we cannot function here, it is unlikely we will be able to function anywhere else. We have before us a most glorious opportunity, that of extending awareness and becoming cooperative agents with the evolutionary energies of nature. Many people are stumbling along through life; just getting by, or hoping to make it through until the grave. What an utterly dismal attitude and what a wasted life! Where are the courageous men and women with vision and imagination? Where are the curious, the willing, the able? Are you one of them? I hope so, for if you are, the world is yours for the taking.

Why is it, if the rules which dictate success are known to all who take the time to study a bit, that not more people are aware and successful? Have you ever wondered? There is only one reason why a person is not successful, if he knows the rules of success—he does not really want to be successful! There can be no other reason. For if a person really wants to reach a goal, is really and truly dedicated to it, he will move heaven and earth to reach it. Nothing will stand in his way. Not tradition. Not lack of education. Not absence of friends or associates. Not oppressive social rules and regulations. Not petty likes and dislikes. Not comfort. Nothing will stand in the way of that person who has single-mindedly determined to be a success!

I am not talking of instant success, though we make amazing progress right from the start. I am talking about assuming the "success consciousness" first and then letting time and experience determine the rest. Think about it; are you really determined to reach your chosen goals? Are you willing to dig, if need be, and sweat and make sacrifices? Are you willing to correct your mistakes and alter your states of consciousness? Are you willing to stop talking and acting like a loser, and begin talking and acting like a winner? Well? Only you can answer and only you can decide.

Master of Time and Circumstances

One who would be master of time and circumstance must be able to manipulate objects in time and space. That is a fancy way of saying one must be able to handle himself and things according to useful design. If we are attached to things we are in bondage to matter. If we are repelled by material things we are just as much in bondage because our function is restricted. Right use of things—money, machines, products, etc.

—is the way of wisdom. Situations which are the result of our creative acts must be useful and serve a purpose if they are worthy of staying in existence. We should be able to handle situations, projects and organizations objectively. We should be able to start them, keep them going, and stop them when they are no longer useful. We should be able to do all of this with full awareness and with no traumatic emotional involvement. Certainly, no regret when we allow a useless situation, project or organization to dissolve into the void from whence it came.

Everything comes out of space and, eventually, returns to space. Albert Einstein observed this and remarked that space was, therefore, *very mysterious*. Form comes out of formless substance and, in time, changes back to the formless state. Something does not come out of *nothing*. Space is *something* and formless energy is *something*. Surely, forms now exist in subtle states that we have not yet imagined possible. And the possible combination of available forms and situations is almost infinite.

We are not all experts in all fields of endeavor. Some people can initiate projects and get them going. Others can cause a cycle of action to persist by feeding it with attention. Then there are those who are objective enough to examine situations and either change them, or dissolve them, to meet the need. We are not our mental images, therefore, we are not the results of our mental imagery. We are not our situations, projects or creatively formed productions. We should be the masters of mental patterns and of events in time and space.

By using the techniques and methods explained in this book you can initiate projects. It will take determination, attention to details, and continued use of creative imagination to keep the project flourishing. If a project is worthwhile, keep it going. Do not be a quitter, looking for an excuse to fail. When the time comes to change your interests, if the project is still worthwhile, pass it on to someone who will manage it or continue rendering service through it. If it should be dissolved, do it with ease and no regrets.

How do you handle temporary loss? Are you defeated? Are you emotionally disturbed? Or, can you pick up the pieces and begin anew with just as much enthusiasm as you once began? A truly successful person knows that all events and circumstances are but shadows on the screen of time and space, and he is able to maintain this realization even while enthusiastically participating in the game of life. In this manner he is never self-deceived, is always happy and radiantly alive.

Balance, Order and Harmony

The successful person is balanced in all things, lives a well ordered life, and is in harmony with nature's laws. We sometimes read of men who have made a fortune in just a few short years and who are rugged, determined, hard-driving and totally dedicated to their work. Many of these men have truly become attuned to the success principles, are balanced, orderly in their affairs, and in harmony with nature's laws. Some exhibit the trappings of success but are desperate men who are motivated by ego and a fear of failure. One of two things will eventually happen: maturity will dawn and all will be made right in time; or there will be a fall from the pedestal of "false" attainment.

We cannot go contrary to the laws of nature. Our world, as Emerson explained, flows before us and takes our signet and form. Fulfillment is impossible to a one-sided person. Contentment is not to be found in chaos. Happiness cannot be had at the expense of flouting nature's laws of action, rest, diet and useful interchange. When there is balance, order and harmony with the laws of nature then success is assured. We have then built our house upon a rock and nothing shall prevail against it. No, not anything. Things, remember, are projections of consciousness from the invisible realm. Our "firm rock" is our settled consciousness. How then can *things* prevail? They cannot.

Which is most important, imagination or creative activity? Imagination is superior, because without it there would be no activity. And activity alone will not guarantee success. There are millions of hard working poor people and time-driven unfulfilled people. There are people whom we call fine and decent, the "salt of the earth," who are frustrated and unhappy. Imagination can do what activity cannot, but the combination of both imagination and inspired activity is unbeatable.

Good intentions are laudable but are not sufficient. We may mean well but not do well. No, good ideas must be implemented almost as soon as they incubate, or when the time is right. I am not talking about procrastination when I suggest proper timing, for there are certain cycles of natural behavior with which we can cooperate if we know how. There is a time to plant and a time to harvest, a time to initiate action and a time to wait for the more appropriate moment. When we are in tune and our mental radio is clear we automatically possess proper timing and very seldom make mistakes in judgment. Sometimes it seems almost as though matters just take care of themselves.

Breaking Through Psychological Barriers

What to do when we try our best and fail? Is there a way to encourage a trend for the better? Yes, but it takes nerve and discipline. We have to put ourselves on the line and commit ourselves to positive action. *We have to set up a situation where we have to produce!* I am not suggesting that you mortgage your family's future on a single "win or lose" proposition. *I am sug-*

gesting specific goals with specific deadlines. I am suggesting discipline, and a will to win. Start *today,* doing what you plan to do, someday! *Set up a program of planning, activity, exercise, diet, meditation and creative work.* Enroll in that self-improvement course you may have been thinking about. Don't complain that it costs too much money. *If it is worth the price, get the money and take the course! Do something positive.* Buy a set of good inspirational books and read them. Then, *put the worthwhile ideas into practice.* Contact the people you have been planning to contact. Shake yourself out of any routine you may be stagnating in by forcing yourself to do something different. *Get up an hour earlier in the morning to exercise, meditate and plan your day.* If need be, get off by yourself and pray until you break through the mental-emotional shell and are *transformed by the renewing of your mind* and dedicated anew to the high purpose for which you were called to this earth. *Do what you know you have to do to succeed. Don't talk about it. Do it!* If you will do these things you cannot possibly fail.

We need to be disciplined, we need to have knowledge about our creative ventures, and we need to follow-through to the favorable termination of the projects. Knowledge and disciplined action is the sure combination which brings fulfillment. Discipline enables us to conserve energy and then direct it wisely. Sloppy thinking habits, purposeless motion, and wasted energy assures defeat and death.

We Are Not Alone

As we plan for ourselves, and those close to us, we should also plan for the human family. In this way our mental boundaries are extended, but there is another reason. It is our duty to care for the world in which we live. As long as we are here we are obligated to render useful service, to people and all life forms. Some teachers say, "The more you give, the more you get!" This sometimes seems to work out, but this is not the reason why we should think in terms of the total picture. It is our duty to participate in the life process. It is that simple. I know, some will say, "I'll do my share when I become successful and can afford it." Others will say, "OK, if you think it will help me prosper." The world needs "our share" now; hoping to prosper as a result of giving to life is a selfish attitude. Why not be mature and perform the duty before you?

It is not easy to serve mankind. Ask anyone who has thought about it, and tried it. Simply writing a check for whatever charitable cause is at hand is not serving intelligently. Giving a few dollars a year to the church of your choice is not rendering useful service. Think about it—how can you really serve your fellow-man and your world? What unique way can you share in the process of world betterment and consciousness transformation?

Today, this moment, can be of prime importance. A decision can be made now that can change the course of your future. It is true that most people are *wiser than they know and better than they usually are.* What is true for one person, regarding the success potential, is true for each one of us. And, the beautiful thing is, we are all destined for fulfillment.

Remember:

1. There is a firm base upon which real success rests.
2. Be a master of time and circumstances.
3. Learn to start ventures, keep them going, and move on without regret when the time comes.
4. Events and circumstances are but shadows on the screen of time and space.
5. See to balance, order and harmony in life.
6. Break through the psychological barriers with disciplined will.
7. We are not alone in this world—lend a helping hand.

Practical Application

1. Ponder well the material in this chapter. Do not deny the fact that you are what you are because of your present state of consciousness. This is the first step in the direction of maturity and responsible behavior. To assert that we are victims of external causes is to avoid self-confrontation and delay positive action.

2. *Projects:* Initiate a minor venture, or a major one. Examine a current project and streamline it to improve effectiveness. Examine a current project which has outlived its usefulness and dissolve it without fanfare or regret.

3. *Projects:* Tell someone how much he, or she, is appreciated and do something thoughtful for that person. If need be, forgive someone. Or, if need be, forgive yourself. Give some of your time and energy to a useful cause, without strings and without recognition. Give a generous sum of money to help someone, or to spread a useful message.

"The general desirous of winning a battle makes many calculations in his temple beforehand."
                              —Sun Tsu (Chinese general), 500 B.C.

"As we become permanent drunkards by so many separate drinks, so we become saints in the moral, and authorities and experts in the practical and scientific spheres by so many separate acts and hours of working. Let no youth have any anxiety about the upshot of his education whatever line of it may be. If he keeps faithfully busy each hour of the working day he may safely leave the final result to itself. He can with perfect certainty count on waking some fine morning, to find himself one of the competent ones of his generation, in whatever pursuit he may have singled out."
                                        —William James

Chapter Eight

STRAIGHT ANSWERS TO
IMPORTANT QUESTIONS

Some of the most often asked questions are to be found in the following pages. Most questions are due to one of the following: the text has not been carefully examined; all words and phrases are not fully understood; subconscious reluctance to change.

What If I Use the Technique of Creative Imagination and Conditions do Not Change?

If the goal is reasonable and natural, (that is, within your capabilities to handle, and within the framework of natural law) it is as possible for conditions not to change as it is for a thing to be, and not be, at the same time. If the goal is realistic, possible of attainment within the time set, and the technique has been used properly so that you live *from the end,* conditions cannot remain the same; because you are not the same in attitude, consciousness, or manner of relating to your environment. If all conditions are properly observed and the shift in attitude and state of consciousness is made, and maintained, this is a process that never fails to bring positive results. Never!

Is One's Age, Sex, or Social Condition a Factor to be Considered Relative to the Use of These Methods and Principles?

All people, regardless of their age, are forever

dreaming dreams into manifestation. Many children do this instinctively until they are conditioned by "older and wiser" people into believing "facts" instead of the truth about the creative process. In teaching others, however, it is well to be sure that the creative methods will be used constructively, regardless of the age of the person who will be using them. Young people can be encouraged to "expect" to do better at their studies, and they will. They can be encouraged to "expect" the best from the world in which they live and the best will be theirs. Above all, with children, do not let them be brainwashed and mentally and emotionally crippled. Teach them to be practical, without taking away their capacity to dream.

Male or female, it matters not, as far as the ability to set and reach goals. Again, one must be reasonable in all respects and be sure the goals set are really what one wants. Career women, working women, wives, young women just starting out in life—nothing restricts you. *The world is a reflection of our states of consciousness.* This is true, regardless of the opinions and theories to the contrary.

One's present social, racial, or cultural background is not a barrier to success: as long as you are willing to work impersonally with the creative principles; not make excuses; and be bold enough to make decisive moves when necessary. The law is, *the world is a reflection of our states of consciousness.* This principle never changes. Therefore, circumstances, or outer appearances and conditions, are temporary. They must give way to superior mental states and disciplined behavior.

What If My Project, When Completed, Is Not Up to My Personal Expectations?

If the imagined conditions are not fully externalized on the screen of time and space it means: the goal was not realistic (that is, not attainable within the framework of natural law or within the time-span set); you settled for less than the ideal condition; the technique was not used properly. Carefully go over the planning stages and the steps in following-through. Is your goal reasonable, and possible of attainment? Are you willing to be disciplined enough not to settle for less than perfection? Have you made the transition, in attitude and consciousness, from looking *at* the goal to living *in* the finished situation, in your mind and consciousness?

How Do We Know We Are Not Where We Are for A Specific Purpose? How Can We Tell The Difference Between God's Will and Our Will?

This is an important question because many people are not responsible and do not want to do their duty in life. We should fulfill our responsibilities to the best of our ability, once we arrive at an understanding as to what they are. We are in the situation in life which we have accepted because of our inner mental states, previous desires, needs for challenge, and because we are just human. It may be that right where we are is where we belong and where we can serve best. If so, the principles of mind and consciousness will enable us to serve most effectively. But, we should be honest with ourselves, after careful examination of our inner states. And be sure that we are not merely accepting a limited situation in life because we lack initiative; feel unworthy or because we are just plain lazy.

As to the question of God's will. What Christians call the *will of God*, by the Hindus is called the dharma or "way of righteousness," and by philosophers "the evolutionary plan of life." Life is playing all of the roles in this manifest realm. Life is even playing the role of the most miserable person. Our lifestyle depends pretty much on us; not upon an external whim. We have the

potential within us to unveil the splendor and glory of
the Divine Principle, if we will but allow it to unfold.
I stress "allowing" because, in most people, this innate
essence is repressed as a result of tension and lack of
self-acceptance. If you need scriptural support then
believe the words of Jesus: "I have come that you
might have life, and have it more abundantly!" But,
whatever your accepted style and manner of living, if
you have accepted it, be happy. Be cheerful and pro-
ductive. Do not complain, justify, or become neurotic
and sick.

Only lack of the will to use imagination keeps us in
bondage, regardless of the circumstance. There are
people whose families have lived in the ghetto, the dead
mining towns, the impoverished areas, who will not
move away from the area because it is "home" to
them. They allow themselves to be victims of circumstances. Others remain in bondage because they accept
the mental restrictions imposed upon them by family
and friends. "I've always believed this way," they say,
"and I always will!"

Can I Be Controlled or Used By Others?
Can I Influence Other People?

All passive people are forever coming under the
enchantments of those who project vivid mental pictures. We are influenced by the environment; by what
we read and hear; by how we react to sense perceived
situations; and by the silent intentions of other people.
Most people do not initiate thought or action, they react
to external challenge or suggestion. As we become
more aware and more objective, we react less and less.
Instead, we *respond* intelligently.

If others are trying to manipulate us by using persuasion and mental influence, we can be free of their
efforts by merely refusing to accept their intentions.
We do not have to build a wall of mental, or psychic,
defense; we have but to be so clear in mind and con-

sciousness that there is nothing in us to which their intentions can relate.

Influencing others is a major responsibility. Even most enlightened people I know will not interfere with another person's life unless specifically invited to do so. We must be careful that we do not meddle in the private affairs of other people. Ask yourself the question: "What right do I have to control or persuade another person?" To dominate another person for personal gain, or satisfaction, is to be selfish. In working with others, bring forth the highest and best of which they are capable of expressing at the moment. In working with children, expect the best and give encouragement and mental, emotional and spiritual support. In working with friends and associates, expect the best and relate in a mature manner. In working with a client, patient, or person whom you are serving, serve the very best you can and work for the most ideal condition your relationship will allow. *Bring forth* the best; do not superimpose your will, or restricted views, on others. Never use another person for personal gain, or personal satisfaction. Let your relationships be a matter of mutual enjoyment and value.

How Do I Know What Is Right or Best for Me?

We begin from where we are by turning within and asking for guidance: "Why am I here?; What are my talents and how can I best use them?; How can I best serve my fellowman?" Use the technique of creative imagination and, in your mind's eye, see a trusted friend and hear that friend say, "I'm so happy to know you have found your right place in life!" Then, respond with mental conversation and *feeling*, and express your gratitude and satisfaction concerning your fulfilled condition. *If you feel fulfilled, then outer conditions must reflect this realization.* By using this process we stimulate guidance, and powers of recognition and decision. We may not always know what is best in the long run, but we can always *do* the best we can moment to moment.

Should I Tell Friends and Associates About My Dreams?

Tell no one except those who will be helpful in the realization of your goals, and those who will be affected in some way. Do not talk about your dreams to people who have no influence to assist you, or who may tend to either change your mind or confuse you. Let things unfold from within the depths of consciousnesss. What is envisioned in secret will be revealed openly. This is true. Do not indulge in idle talk, waste energy on speculation, or drain your energies. Conserve mental power and spiritual resources and let them be directed intelligently. Be disciplined at all times. If you waver in your faith: either talk with a trusted friend; read inspirational material; reinforce your attitude by practicing the technique again; or do something to keep your hopes up and your assurance strong and steady. *Believe!* Pray and *believe*, picture and *accept*.

Is There the Possibility of Creating Unwanted or Undesirable Future Conditions?

Some people will not use these creative methods because they are afraid of binding themselves to the future by creating unwanted, or painful, situations. If we are objective and mature we will always be fully aware of the process and responsible for whatever happens. If what unfolds is not to our liking, or outlives its usefulness, we will simply dissolve it or move into a more acceptable set of circumstances. We must use the mind as long as we function in time and space. The challenge is to use it wisely, and with full control over mental imagery. Since we may not be knowledgeable, or mature, when we begin to use these methods it is likely that we will bring together situations which are in need of improvement, or are not really useful. This cannot be avoided and we can mark it up to experience. The major points are, be *aware* and be *responsible.*

Does One Have to Be a Good Person To Derive Benefits from These Methods?

"Good" means different things to different people. One should be *ethical* and *moral* in all relationships: because it is the honest way to be; it guarantees a clear consciousness and a distortion-free mind; and because *we attract to ourselves that which we can believe to be true about others.* We do not want any negative or limited mental-emotional condition in our consciousness if we can possibly help it.

If we are ethical, moral, and healthy-minded regarding our relationships with life in general, we are likely to be more balanced and happy. Personal habits can be categorized as those which are useful, and those which are not useful. Or, those which are constructive, and those which are destructive. Good and bad need not enter in; merely what is useful and constructive vs. that which is not useful.

Concerning Revision: Is it Really Possible to Alter the Past?

We, of course, do not change the past happenings. We alter the emotional content of the memory-pictures so they no longer influence us. We retain full access to the memories of past experiences but we can remain objective as we scan them. Because of this we do not mistake the present for the past. *Superimposition* is a major problem for many people; that is, they impose upon a present-time situation the opinions and feelings of a similar past-situation, instead of dealing with a present-time situation for what it is. Sometimes present situations are *just like* past ones, because our consciousness tends to cause patterns to be duplicated, unless we change our state of consciousness. If our level of awareness changes and our state of consciousness changes, and we remove the emotion from memories, we can "live in the present" with full powers of perception and function.

Is It Possible to Become so Involved With the Creative Process That We Live In Fantasy Instead of Reality?

Even imagined states are real, of course, but one who lives in fantasy is usually daydreaming or just "floating" mentally in order to escape confronting the reality of this world. We have already stressed the importance of responsible relationships, of mental and emotional maturity, and of working in harmony with the Life Process. As we follow through properly we find ourselves more and more in touch with reality, or life as it expresses and unfolds. It stands to reason that we should not encourage people who are mentally or emotionally unstable to use these procedures: the exceptions being that we show them how to *see* themselves balanced and functional; and we refrain from encouraging them to become "spaced out," and out of touch with this-world reality.

Is It Necessary To Make Sacrifices To Insure Success? Or, Pay for What We Want?

Rather than think in terms of sacrifice, think in terms of discipline. We must, of course, give up attitudes, states of consciousness, energy-wasting activities, and all which has no bearing on our goals if we are to be successful in the quickest possible time. This is a matter of being efficient and of making intelligent use of what we have to work with. Payment will be in service we render and in giving up everything which stands in the way of fulfillment. The decision is ours.

What is it you want from life? Pay for it and take it.

What If Friends and Family Do Not Understand, or Go Along With, My Ideals and Principles?

We are allowed our private life. Do not share your dreams and ideals with those who do not understand or appreciate them. One need not feel out-of-step with life because of having been awakened to the awareness of natural laws which are not readily discerned by others. Practice in privacy and do not dramatize your disciplines. Let your transformed life be the sermon. While it is nice to have the emotional support of family and friends, it is not absolutely essential. You are too big to complain that others do not understand you.

If associates are oppressive and destructive, and will not help themselves, you may be inclined to break off your relationship. Or, at least establish guidelines for the relationship so that you will not be prevented from fulfilling your destiny. Under any and all circumstances, do the best you possibly can. No one can expect more.

"Of all the beautiful truths pertaining to the soul which have been restored and brought to light in this Age, none is more gladdening or fruitful of divine promise and confidence than this—that man is the master of thought, the moulder of character, and the maker and shaper of condition, environment and destiny."

—As A Man Thinketh
James Allen

NOTES

Share This Book With Friends and Associates

How You Can Use The Technique of Creative Imagination is the ideal book to give to a friend who needs a boost, a high school or college student just beginning to embark upon life's great adventure, or to a business associate.

Obtain this title from your usual distributor or from us by mail. Organizations, dealers, heads of groups—can order in quantity at special discounts. Write for information to:

CSA Press
Lakemont, Georgia 30552

Free catalog of available titles and recordings available upon request. A postcard will do.

NOTES

NOTES

NOTES